OWNSEND   BAEDEKER   GEORGE BANCROF   IN FINLEY

NEDY   HENRY WARD BEECHER   JA   ELL LOWELL

THORNE   STEPHEN VINCENT BENÉT   RUDYARD KIPLING

D KIPLING   HENRY BESTON   EDWIN ARLINGTON ROBINSON

S. ELIOT   WILLIAM BRADFORD   HERMAN MELVILLE

ELLOW   SINCLAIR LEWIS   JOHN GREENLEAF WHITTIER

E JEWETT   VAN WYCK BROOKS   RALPH WALDO EMERSON

BRADLEY   ROLLO WALTER BROWN   FERRIS GREENSLET

CATHER   EDWARD S. BURGESS   HENRY DAVID THOREAU

EL WEBSTER   RACHEL CARSON   CHARLES WENDELL TOWNSEND

HAWAY   MARY ELLEN CHASE   NATHANIEL HAWTHORNE

R   MASON FITCH COGSWELL   OLIVER WENDELL HOLMES, JR.

G. HINE   WILBUR L. CROSS   STEPHEN VINCENT BENÉT

RY BESTON   BERNARD DeVOTO   ANNIE TRUMBULL SLOSSON

R LEWIS   EMILY DICKINSON   ARTHUR STANLEY PEASE

OMAS HILL   CHARLES DUNN, JR.   EDWARD MARTIN TABER

NEW ENGLAND REVISITED

A Photographic Study by Arthur Griffin

Curtis B. Ford, C.L.U.

Pioneer Valley ~ Hartford C.L.U. Seminar

May 2, 1978

With Thanks

ARTHUR GRIFFIN'S
NEW

With descriptions chosen & edited

by DAVID McCORD

ENGLAND REVISITED

ARTHUR GRIFFIN · EUCLID AVENUE · WINCHESTER · MASS

For the use of selections from copyrighted material, the editors are indebted to the following publishers and copyright proprietors:

APPLETON-CENTURY-CROFTS, INC.: *I Travel by Train* by Rollo Walter Brown; copyright 1939 by D. Appleton Century & Co., Inc.

BRANDT & BRANDT: *Western Star* by Stephen Vincent Benét; Holt, Rinehart & Winston, Inc.; copyright 1943 by Rosemary Carr Benét; reprinted by permission of Brandt & Brandt.

BROWN, JAMES, ASSOCIATES, INC.: *Flowering Earth* by Donald Culross Peattie; copyright 1939 by Donald Culross Peattie; reprinted by permission of the Author's Estate and its agent, James Brown Associates, Inc.

CHISWICK PRESS, THE: *Fishing in New England* by Leslie P. Thompson.

COWARD-McCANN, INC.: *The Little Locksmith* by Katherine Butler Hathaway; copyright 1942, 1943 by Coward-McCann; reprinted by permission of the publisher.

DeVOTO, AVIS: *New England: There She Stands* by Bernard DeVoto; reprinted with the permission of Mrs. DeVoto.

DOUBLEDAY & COMPANY, INC.: *Herbs and the Earth* by Henry Beston; copyright 1935 by Doubleday & Company, Inc.; reprinted by permission of the publisher. *Letters of Travel* by Rudyard Kipling; reprinted by permission of the publisher and of Mrs. George Bambridge.

DUTTON, E. P., & Co., INC.: *The Flowering of New England* by Van Wyck Brooks; copyright 1936, 1952 by Van Wyck Brooks and ©1964 by Gladys Brooks; reprinted by permission of E. P. Dutton & Co., Inc.

GALLOWS HILL PRESS: *Waumbek Junction* by Arthur Stanley Pease.

HARPER AND ROW: *The Sense of Wonder* by Rachel Carson; excerpts from pp. 42, 43, and 45; copyright ©1965 by Rachel L. Carson; reprinted by permission of the publisher.

HARVARD UNIVERSITY PRESS: *The Harvard Book* ed. by William Bentink-Smith; *Sequestered Vales of Life* by Arthur Stanley Pease; *On Occasion* by David McCord; reprinted by permission of the publisher.

HOLT, RINEHART AND WINSTON, INC.: *Complete Poems of Robert Frost*; "Spring Pools" copyright 1928 by Holt, Rinehart and Winston, Inc. copyright © 1956 by Robert Frost; "New Hampshire" copyright 1923 by Holt, Rinehart and Winston, Inc., copyright 1951 by Robert Frost. *The Outermost House* by Henry Beston; copyright 1928, 1949, ©1956 by Henry Beston. *A Northern Countryside* by Rosalind Richards; copyright 1916 by Holt, Rinehart and Winston, Inc., copyright 1944 by Rosalind Richards. *A Goodly Heritage* by Mary Ellen Chase; copyright 1932, ©1960 by Mary Ellen Chase; reprinted with the permission of Holt, Rinehart and Winston, Inc.

KNOPF, ALFRED A., INC.: *Modern Prints and Drawings*, ed. by Paul J. Sachs; copyright 1954 by Paul J. Sachs; reprinted by permission of Alfred A. Knopf, Inc.

LIPPINCOTT, J. B., CO.: *Willa Cather: A Memoir* by Elizabeth Shepley Sergeant; copyright 1953 by Elizabeth Shepley Sergeant.

MACMILLAN COMPANY, THE: *Man Against the Sky* by Edward Arlington Robinson; copyright 1916 by E. A. Robinson, copyright 1942 by Ruth Nivison; reprinted with the permission of The Macmillan Company.

MARSHALL JONES COMPANY: *Beach Grass* by Charles Wendell Townsend; reprinted with the permission of the publishers.

McNALLY, RAND, & COMPANY: *Justin Morgan Had a Horse* by Marguerite Henry; copyright 1945 by Marguerite Henry; reprinted by permission of the author and Rand McNally & Co.

SCRIBNER'S, CHARLES, SONS: *The Crows* by David McCord; reprinted with the permission of the publishers.

Affectionately Dedicated
to My Daughter

LEE

Who Designed this Book for Me

Book and Jacket Design by Lee Griffin

All Color Photographs made on KODAK Ektachrome Daylight Film

Color Lithography by the Case-Hoyt Corporation Rochester N.Y.

Color Prints on Warren Cameo Brilliant Dull

Jacket Warren Lustro Offset Enamel Gloss Plasticoted

Text and Endpapers Lithographed by Spencer Press Boston

Endpapers Strathmore Grandee Special Color

*Text Pages Gray Laid Fairmont Offset Vellum Finish by
                    Tileston and Hollingsworth*

Composition on Photon by Machine Composition Company Boston

Binding Cloth Holliston Record Buckram Special Color

Hand-bound by the College Bindery South Lancaster Massachusetts

Prologue

It is only when we are aware of the earth and of the earth as poetry that we truly live. Ages and people which sever the earth from the poetic spirit, or do not care, or stop their ears with knowledge as with dust, find their veins grown hollow and their hearts an emptiness echoing to questioning. For the earth is ever more than the earth, more than the upper and the lower field, the tree and the hill. Here is mystery banded about the forehead with green, here are gods ascending, here is benignancy and the corn in the sun, here terror and night, here life, here death, here fire, here the wave coursing in the sea. It is this earth which is the true inheritance of man, his link with his human past, the source of his religion, ritual and song, the kingdom without whose splendour he lapses from his mysterious estate of man to a baser world which is without the other virtue and the other integrity of the animal. True humanity is no inherent right but an achievement; and only through the earth may we be as one with all who have been and all who are yet to be, sharers and partakers of the mystery of living, reaching to the full of human peace and the full of human joy.

HENRY BESTON

Foreword

Beauty is said to be in the eye of the beholder. If this be true, the educated eye will recognize interesting and beautiful photographs at a glance. In landscape alone, thousands of them are taken every year in every state of the Union.

The New England area, however, offers more varied subjects than any other part of the country. For New England is a more closely packed slice of history. There has been a great deal of concentrated living in its collected states; these years and years of people and the kaleidoscope of their experiences are preserved everywhere to lure the discerning eye and the recorder of natural grace and wonder.

New England, too, is blessed with a tremendous variety of scenery, all contained in its relatively convenient economy-sized package. Its ocean shore is lined with dramatic rocks against which the waves play an obliging discordant ballet, while but a short distance away, the water washes more politely against sand dunes and gentle beaches. Just round the corner, the boats of the fishing fleet, or the yachts of the leisured, invite a still further fascinating investigation.

New England, of course, is bounded only on one side by the ocean. Its interior is a richly varied treasure-trove of the picturesque, some with the mark of a past generation, some with the bright bustle of modern technology. Woods, fields, streams, lakes, mountains, and valleys are set as upon a stage awaiting the pleasure of one's viewing and the capture of the experience on film.

In fact, New England is almost a cliché. From the "rock-ribbed coast" of Maine to the "rolling Berkshires" at the New York State line, New England looks like one big picture postcard. But let the sophisticated beware, for Maine *is* rock-ribbed, and the Berkshires *do* roll, and those covered bridges are very real indeed, built in one particular way for one particular purpose. Likenesses and imitations, elsewhere, are cliché-ridden. New England is the original.

New England probably fascinates the American traveler for psychological reasons too, for it was the source of much which was to develop and become the United States. It is an area which helps satisfy everyone's desire for a sense of continuity, that almost universal need to identify with an ancestral source. This interest in the charm and beauty of history is shown by the national passion for "antiques" and early Americana. All New England was, of course, Early American. Much of it still is.

For each of the past twenty-five years, I have traveled over 25,000 miles on assignment for national magazines and advertisers. Despite this lengthy and continuous look at the rest of the world, I return to New England each time as a coming home. Its small towns and villages have an attraction for me unequalled anywhere else. There are probably few back roads I haven't investigated looking for the picture of the year.

Creating photographs, however, is a little like fishing. First one must locate the fishing pool, then fish at the right time, when the fish are feeding. There is a right time of the day for every picture when the light shows off the place to best advantage. This may be early in the morning, late in the afternoon, or at midday. It may be in a snowstorm or when the rain is descending in buckets. Any time will be suitable for a record. Only the right time serves us for the real picture. Thus, several trips to a given place may be necessary before the ideal picture is captured. If you're lucky, conditions might be perfect the first time. If they are, be pleased; but don't expect it often.

For example, the New Harbor scene on page 93 was photographed at sunrise. Obviously a sunset time would not do because the sun sets in the wrong direction. During midday, the light made the scene flat and just another collection of white boats on blue water. Early in the morning, everything had a warm glow, and the drama I wanted to present.

8

I am aware that the film manufacturers recommend photographing in color only between 10 A.M. and 3 P.M. for true scene reproduction. They are right, because people don't really see color as it is. The average user thinks white is *only* white. White is yellow in the morning because yellow light from a sunrise makes it so. And it may be pink in the evening if it is illuminated by a rosy sky. Go ahead, photograph any time, but learn to *see* what you're looking at, and anticipate a reproduction of what is there.

Another warning of the film makers can be ignored with profit. They suggest taking pictures with the sun behind the photographer. This results in flat lighting. Although it is the easiest to measure, it is the least interesting kind of lighting. Many people merely want records of where they have been, or of the time Uncle Andy visited home. Flat lighting will yield the record with the greatest allowance for error. But if something more than a record is wanted, try to get into some position where the light comes across the scene (cross-lighting) or from the back, so that the sun is in front of the camera. Shield the lens with a lens shade, a hat, or have someone cast a shadow across the lens (without obscuring the scene). And increase exposure 50 to 100 per cent if detail in the darker shadows is important. Photographs made this way will be much more interesting than flat snapshots. A good one will make you feel like a real artist.

It is not the purpose of this book to be a course in picture-making, but many owners of my other all-color book *New England* requested me to include more technical data in this book. I can't resist the opportunity of urging the reader to break a few rules. My "Camera Notes" with the pictures may give you some ideas. Use a little imagination and create something that will not be just a record of a beautiful place. The extra effort and thought will result in something with some of *you* in it. Something you and only you created.

This is exciting and a source of a very fundamental satisfaction.

All of the photographs in this book were made on 4 X 5 Kodak Ektachrome sheet film with the exception of five made on 620 Kodak Ektachrome Roll Film (as recorded in my camera notes). Unless specified I used a 6-inch lens with my camera set firmly on a tripod. All photographs were enlarged without any retouching and only a few were slightly cropped. The amateur, using 35mm equipment, may prefer Kodachrome. It doesn't matter much. I usually use the 4 X 5 because my pictures are meant for reproduction in magazines and books, where the larger size is easier to work with. And, of course, Kodachrome film is not available in large sheets.

As to cameras, the person using them is more important than the equipment. Naturally, the finer the quality, the better the picture from a technical viewpoint. But a perfectly wire-sharp nothing viewpoint is certainly less pleasing—and less successful—than one showing imagination, even if the image does display the softness and slight mushiness of a cheap lens. Get and learn to use the best camera you can afford. But don't despair if all you have is an inexpensive little record-maker. You're the one that can make or break the picture.

This book is a comparatively quick trip through New England even though a lot of effort went into the making of every picture. At best, it can be but a minute sampling of the wonderful photographic subjects offered by this utterly delightful area. And with the changing seasons, every scene presents a different picture. A person can devote a lifetime to New England and never cover half of the possibilities. I know. I have.

Winchester, Massachusetts   *ARTHUR GRIFFIN*
12   September, 1966

CONTENTS

Prologue: Henry Beston

Foreword: Arthur Griffin

Introduction: David McCord

Spring

Summer

CONTENTS

Fall

Winter

Introduction

A book is a measure of the spirit of man; this one an availing complex of the prose and verse of many writers summoned here to support, and in certain places to explain, the work of an artist greatly gifted in the chancy medium of lens and color film. Not that Arthur Griffin's landscapes of New England need another's gloss or postscript; they stand quite brilliantly and proudly on their own. But Mr. Griffin's earlier *New England* was enhanced by a series of essays, each one written to sustain its matching picture. With this in mind, it was decided that *New England Revisited* should draw upon the work of authors and poets no longer living, and that they as a company should supply full commentary. Not all of these authors and poets were to be New Englanders, but you will readily observe that most of them are. While choosing forty-four selections—forty of which appear to windward on a right-hand page and four on a left—the editor suggested the addition of brief notes on every passage chosen, simply and solely to achieve a fugue-like structure for the volume and thereby hold together in one plane divergent scenes and seasons, mountains, valleys, field and forest, lakes and the Atlantic littoral. These supplementary notes appear in Roman type, one each on every left-hand page, facing the picture opposite.

Most important of all, of course, are Mr. Griffin's factual camera data, printed (as they should be) in arresting italics. They tell you where his tripod stood or where the camera was hand-held, give shutter opening, timing, and the like; but better still, they talk about locale, light, weather, hour of the day, with now and then a word on obstacles or dangers overcome. I for one, an Instamatic man, have learned in reading them that afternoon for cross-light is desirable.

One saw right off that wholly to arrest a passage of prose or a series of stanzas suited to the landscape, seascape, or mountain view in question would be not only difficult but impossible. So, first of all, I made a list of sixty writers, each of whom might well provide an item I was looking for. On this half-winnowed list, the obvious names stood out: Emerson, Thoreau, Sarah Orne Jewett, Emily Dickinson,

Robert Frost, Daniel Webster, William Bradford, and so on. With them and into them I began my search, widening out through other names and other books as I became familiar more in detail with the pictures and with certain subtle demands their wide diversity could make. For the old North Bridge in Concord any schoolboy would have chosen Emerson's Hymn. But Emerson invaded many other scenes at many points; Thoreau even more. And every harbor study of the rough Maine Coast suggested Miss Jewett. A beginning was made; but from then on, on his own, the editor had warily to edge his way.

I wanted above all to get the *feel* of color into type. States talk a private language. Often some sure passage came to light, only to kill itself because the season was wrong, the tone at variance with what the tone of the total book should be, or because something queer or extraneous intruded itself at just the wrong right-angle turn of phrase. Certain compromises soon were obvious. With *Mayflower II* under sail in replica, 100 miles from Plymouth waters, the time was summer; but unfortunately the words of William Bradford were converging on me at the edge of winter. John Finley's warm reflection on those drops of water from Assisi emptied into a New Hampshire spring could reasonably expect pictorial balance in the Granite State. The best I could do with it was to place the passage out of state, but opening on a view of the distant Presidentials. I expect, however, that Mr. Finley had his Tamworth or at least the Sandwich intervales in mind.

Nor did Thoreau, unless I have misread him, ever do his walking in Connecticut. Nevertheless, his aphoristic observations, as I shuffled them together, *did* include the dogwood. Last of all, those several remnants of fine English in its third harmonic, carefully culled from all that is recorded of Bill Pratt, philosopher of Williamstown. How well, I hope the reader will agree, they match the arcane mystery of Katahdin Falls as Mr. Griffin took them in.

With some of my originals I parted all uneasy lest my choices here or there had not done justice to the subject. It would take a volume twenty times this size to utilize the wealth and range of New England letters. *Ab uno disce omnes.* Here I cannot fail to call on one to speak for all and sway the reader toward Plum Island and the spring-tide 17th century prose of old Judge Samuel Sewall. What marvellous music and a matchless sense was his:

> As long as the Sea-Fowl shall know the Time of their coming, and not neglect seasonably to visit the Places of their Acquaintance . . . As long as any free & harmless Doves shall find a White Oak, or other Tree within the Township, to perch, or feed, or build a careless Nest upon; and shall voluntarily present themselves to perform the office of Gleaners after Barley-Harvest; As long as Nature shall not grow Old and dote; but shall constantly remember to give the rows of Indian Corn their education, by Pairs: So long shall Christians be born there. . . .

New England, so it seems to me, is the authorized version of America. Perhaps only a New Yorker raised at the rainy end of the Oregon Trail can say as much and say it with true feeling. There she is: six states, six countries all in one. Six states that share in landscape, much as Everyman his backdrop of an evening sky or dawn ascending from the sea, unfold. This is the map of New England which filling stations can't supply. This is the map of New England: she who gave us villages and cities, chimneyed well and mitred cunningly as though white pine were teakwood; slanting fields all tilled or ravened where the stone walls roll through juniper, tall wayward dunes along the Cape, the questing headlands far down East, some matchless mountains green or white, sweet valleys half morainal, half a sanctuary.

So if anything at all, the borrowed writing in this book does stand with Henry Beston "on the side of life." Each paragraph or couplet, unrelated as it islands small in voice and rhythm, dream and waking, speaks aloud the ancient word of man upon his earth. It isn't therapy; it hints at no escape; but something deeper where the roots go down, the cumulus sails seaward, and the light is on the land.

DAVID MCCORD

13

SPRING

Orchard Voices

My fancy has always found something very interesting in an orchard—especially an old orchard. Apple-trees, and all fruit-trees, have a domestic character, which brings them into relationship with man; they have lost, in a great measure, the wild nature of the forest-tree, and have grown humanized, by receiving the care of man, and by contributing to his wants. They have become a part of the family; and their individual characters are as well understood and appreciated as those of the human members. One tree is harsh and crabbed—another mild—one is churlish and illiberal—another exhausts itself with its free-hearted bounties. Even the shapes of apple-trees have great individuality, into such strange postures do they put themselves, and thrust their contorted branches so grotesquely in all directions. And when they have stood around a house for many years, and held converse with successive dynasties of occupants, and gladdened their hearts so often in the fruitful autumn, then it would seem almost sacrilege to cut them down. . . .

NATHANIEL HAWTHORNE

Of "shunning men and women," they talk of hallowed things, aloud, and embarrass my dog. He and I don't object to them, if they'll exist their side. I think Carl would please you. He is dumb, and brave. I think you would like the chestnut tree I met in my walk. It hit my notice suddenly, and I thought the skies were in blossom.

Then there's a noiseless noise in the orchard that I let persons hear.

You told me in one letter you could not come to see me "now," and I made no answer; not because I had none, but did not think myself the price that you should come so far.

I do not ask so large a pleasure, lest you might deny me.

You say, "Beyond your knowledge." You would not jest with me, because I believe you; but, preceptor, you cannot mean it?

All men say "What" to me, but I thought it a fashion.

When much in the woods, as a little girl, I was told that the snake would bite me, that I might pick a poisonous flower, or goblins kidnap me; but I went along and met no one but angels, who were far shyer of me than I could be of them, so I haven't that confidence in fraud which many exercise.

I shall observe your precept, though I don't understand it, always.

I marked a line in one verse, because I met it after I made it, and never consciously touch a paint mixed by another person.

I do not let go it, because it is mine. Have you the portrait of Mrs. Browning?

Persons sent me three. If you had none, will you have mine?

EMILY DICKINSON

There was never any prose remotely like that of Emily Dickinson at her high-level best. Here is a fragment of another letter—to another person on another subject—exquisite as those apple blossoms on the next page, which might well caption the whole twelve seasons in the compass of this book:

"I send a violet, for L——. I should have sent a stem, but was overtaken by snow-drifts. I regret deeply not to add a butterfly, but have lost my hat, which precludes my catching one."

NORTH POMFRET, VERMONT

*Spring in Vermont arrives gently, with the first
thaws ushering in the sugaring season (see page
27). Then, about mid-May apple-blossoms burst
fully into bloom. I return to this little pool year
after year in the spring, shooting pictures, but I
have never done any as fine as this one. The ripple
in the foreground was made by a stone. Sometimes
nature needs a little help! North Pomfret lies in
the upland a few miles north of Woodstock through
a region of smooth-rolling hills. This pool is at
an altitude of some 1200 feet.*

*Note for real camera fans: It is nice that this
double-spread picture happens to be the first in my
book, for it is a good example of framing a scene.
When I made this picture I had no idea that I
might have to crop the top and bottom to fit this
unusual size. I didn't care to crop the ripples, but
if I didn't I couldn't show the top of the barn.
What to do? As I was having the same scene on the
back of the jacket, I decided to show the ripples
in this picture and the top of the barn on the jacket.
Incidentally, this and the other three seasonal
spreads are the only pictures which are cropped.
All the others show the full transparency, for when
I set the camera on the tripod, I compose the
picture as I want it to be reproduced.*

Exposure—1/25 of a second at f:16. ASA Speed 50.

18

Spring Pools

These pools that, though in forests, still reflect
The total sky almost without defect,
And like the flowers beside them, chill and shiver,
Will like the flowers beside them soon be gone,
And yet not out by any brook or river,
But up by roots to bring dark foliage on.

The trees that have it in their pent-up buds
To darken nature and be summer woods—
Let them think twice before they use their powers
To blot out and drink up and sweep away
These flowery waters and these watery flowers
From snow that melted only yesterday.

ROBERT FROST

"Spring Pools" is surely one of Robert Frost's most delicate yet strongly satisfying lyrics. Observe the inner strength of the first stanza at the moment where the poet repeats "the flowers beside them"; and then how he plays with this simple device by repeating himself again in the second stanza— but now in reverse: "these flowery waters and these watery flowers." This is the way in which all unobtrusively he brings reflection into the poem just as weather and the camera's lens bring it into the picture. The poet has to be in focus too.

EAST BETHEL, VERMONT

You could also call this winter's final gasp. I was up in Stowe to get the last of snow studies in early April, but they had a thaw and no sun for almost a week, so I headed for home. Driving down route 14 toward White River Junction I came upon this foggy scene. I didn't then think too much of it, but feeling that I just had to get something for my week's waiting in Stowe, I took it. The Saturday Evening Post *used it for a double page spread.*

Exposure—1/25 of a second at f:14. ASA Speed 50.

ARTHUR GRIFFIN

Sugaring Off

And now the big barnyard gate swings wide as the Farm Boy with a wave of his goad-stick and a brief "Wo-hoish" starts toward the ox-sled, followed by his team. The off ox steps across the sled-tongue, and they range up side by side while the end of the sled-tongue is slipped through the yoke-ring and the iron clevis-pin drops into place. A log-chain is hooked just above the yoke-ring and the other end of the chain made fast to the iron hook on the top of the tongue-roller of the sled and "Wo-hoish Buck, haw Broad"—a ton and a half of ox-beef is thrust against the bows and yoke.—Nothing happens. The heavy sled remains stationary. Ah, the steel sled-shoves are frozen fast by sub-zero nights to the snow beneath them. A direct pull fails to loosen them. So: "Back Buck, haw Broad here!" with a wave of the goad-stick across Buck's face and a swing across Broad's back, there is a powerful left swing of the sled-tongue and a sidewise motion of the sled which wrenches the runners loose from the snow, and everything is moving. Around behind the big barn there has been no track for all winter. Snow, however, is not very deep there, for the wind eddying around the big building has blown a lot of it away. Two feet, perhaps, remained; but oxen can wallow, how they can wallow! Pulling out the clevis-pin and unhooking the chain from the yoke, leaving the sled standing, the Farm Boy, taking a shovel, marked out two tracks through the snow leading out around and coming back alongside the smoke-house. Then the oxen in response to his "Wo-hoish! Come on boys!" followed him around two or three times, crushing down the snow until a good track was made for the sled which, presently, was halted alongside the smoke-house. Just then the tall form of the Farmer, wearing a gray home-spun frock, cap and mittens, appeared around the corner of the barn. "Want any help, Sonny?" he shouted against the wind. "No, sir, I can handle it all right."

CHARLES DUNN, JR.

The shallow copper dish in front of me, shaped like the larger black one I used for panning gold on my uncle's Oregon ranch, contains a number of curious objects bedded down on a couple of hundred paper clips: a piece of petrified wood, an Oregon thunder-egg showing on one side the polished surface of a pale blue crystal, a fine thick copper ring once inserted in the nose of a bull, a brass lobster ping-pong prize from an old Cunard Steamship, an Indian artifact for scraping skins, a piece of Italian movable type, and a small bright metal spile from Vermont.

Spile and staddle are two unusual words which I associate with New England. Those driven trunks of trees in a salt water marsh, arranged in a circle like a fairy stonehenge only a couple of feet or so in height, are staddles, put there to support, bone dry, a mushroom mound of hay. Spiles are driven into sugar maples to drain off the sap. Sitting by a cemetery one spring-thaw day in Vermont, I watched the drip of sap from a metal spile and wondered if I could not effect an equation, timing the flow of drops, whereby one could estimate the outdoor temperature by the frequency of the drops just as we can do this by counting the number of cricket chirps per minute. It is the thrifty Vermonter who taps his maples just inside the cemetery wall so that all the spiles are hidden from the road. I have not failed to observe that sap buckets hung thereon are notably small economy size. How pleasant to pour fresh maple syrup when the sugaring-off was done where roots run deep among the friendly country of the dead. One can think of far worse fates than being buried, as it were, in a sugar orchard.

One note on the oxen: more than thirty years ago I walked one day with Henry Beston—the second man I ever saw to walk in shorts this side of Europe—somewhere along the route of the old Narrow Gauge Railroad which ran from Wiscassett to Rangeley. We stopped, I remember, in a tiny village store, the kind in which you feel instantly at home. I remember buying two ox goads: pale slender shafts, likely of ash, with a sharp metal point at one end. I have long since lost the two of them; but during their lifetime, I used one or another as a probe and walking stick in whatever turbulent wild stream I happened to be fishing. I had never seen one for sale before, nor have I since.

BRISTOL, NEW HAMPSHIRE

The running of the sap heralds the first signs of spring. There is plenty of maple sugaring still being done in the hills of New Hampshire. The sap runs best in the maple trees during a mild day after a night of freezing cold. From the "orchard" the sap will be hauled to the sugar house where an average of thirty gallons of it will be boiled down to one gallon of syrup. The farmers are very long suffering of tourists and camera fans. Equip yourself with a good supply of film and wear warm waterproof footwear because there will be mud on some of the gravel roads. In years of spring-shooting my car has been hauled out of axle deep mud by oxen, horses, and tractors.

Exposure—1/25 of a second at f:16. ASA Speed 50.

ARTHUR GRIFFIN

Monadnock Region

Willa Cather was buried in the Old Cemetery, Jaffrey Center, New Hampshire. The New England pioneers who incorporated this village in 1773 are said to have "raised" the framework of their enormous church, known as "the Old Meeting House," on the day of the Battle of Bunker Hill. The Old Meeting House stands on a height and dominates the intimate village square, with its old spreading trees, charming old houses, some white, some rosy brick. Beyond the high white edifice, toward Monadnock Mountain, the Old Burying ground slopes steeply down, like Thornton Wilder's graveyard in *Our Town*. There lie the early settlers, under their delicately engraved grey stones and monuments. Willa's grave, with its pure white, graciously curved headstone, is the very last near the lower fence with no other between it and the view, and seems to hang suspended above a flat, blue space of sky and level, forest-grown plain stretching to the long humped Roman profile of Monadnock.

"Don't you feel she must be lonely here?" asked a young writer who was with me on one occasion when I visited the grave from Peterborough.

No lonelier than she was anyhow, I answered, when she committed herself to the impersonal life of the novelist which seemed to mean much more to her than her personal life. In Jaffrey she had worked on some of her finest books, and her spiritual home, so I imagined, was, indeed, the place where she wrote at her best.

The words carved in a lower corner of the stone seem almost to be *spoken* in a low, familiar voice:

. . . *That is happiness; to be dissolved into something complete and great.*

The quotation concludes the fervent, earthy chapter of *My Antonia* in which the little boy first observes and experiences the prairie after he reaches his grandmother's homestead near Black Hawk. Jim was entirely happy, walking through the red, blowing grass to the edge of the world, feeling the "motion" in the country which seemed "somehow to be running." He sat down among his grandmother's pumpkins on the warm earth of the draw bottom.

"Perhaps we feel like that when we die and become a part of something entire, whether it is sun and air, or goodness and knowledge."

ELIZABETH SHEPLEY SERGEANT

If you have missed *My Ántonia*, first published in 1918, you have missed a work of genius. Not to read it is like not reading *Huckleberry Finn* or *The Country of the Pointed Firs*.

A whole book could be written about Monadnock and the almost legion of writers, painters, and musicians it has nourished and inspired. In this book itself we have Edwin Arlington Robinson, Willa Cather, Elizabeth Shepley Sergeant, Rollo Walter Brown, and perhaps one or two others who have fitted easily into that proud canton of lower New Hampshire. Two others, anyway, are Abbott Thayer, the painter, and Louis Agassiz Fuertes, one of the handful of great artists who have devoted their lives to the drawing and painting of wild birds. Fuertes, like Edward Martin Taber, was a pupil of Thayer. Thayer's son, Gerald, "his most devoted, sympathetic, and acute critic," never relented in his effort to persuade Fuertes to paint birds against true backgrounds. Fuertes objected that the doctrine of concealing coloration if carried to a logical end would conceal the bird from the beholder. It was Abbott Thayer who "wore himself out trying to get the Allies to concealingly color their ships and men" in World War I. In a letter to Fuertes, dated Monadnock: 28 February 1917, Mrs. Thayer reports second-hand on the universal camouflage at the French front. "But all this came too late," she says . . . "to save Abbott from getting so worn out that, though he has been sick a year now, he seems to make very little progress toward health."

Earlier (Monadnock, N. H., Jan., 1917), Abbott Thayer himself had written to Fuertes:

"If I were God and had painted those past-all-human-painter-powers true landscapes on the animal world I should enjoy seeing Louis Fuertes reveal the fact. The fact that a *woodcock* could sit on top of a church steeple doesn't make it either art or science to paint him there. It is the vast averages that art perpetuates. You are going to see the Am. Museum *et al* look pretty cheap, with most, all Europe following me, and merely through *studying* me.

I am coming out, soon, with a perfectly astounding confirmation of all my conceal[ing] col[oration] business. No one can know what a grief it is to me that your beautiful pictures are not devoted to their revelations.

But if you don't see them you can't of course, *do* them."

(Abbott Thayer)

MOUNT MONADNOCK, NEW HAMPSHIRE

For many years I had tried to get an interesting picture of this rugged masculine outline (alt. 3166). This mountain stands alone. . . . Called an "airy citadel" by Emerson, it has the stern quality of a fortress, battered by long centuries of exposure to wind and ice. Thoreau, Emerson and others of the Concord writers would board the train in Concord, get off at Troy and climb this mountain. Late one spring day I came upon these three white geese in Perkins Pond. After a few hours of waiting and a few loaves of bread, I managed to come up with this composition. I have found the Monadnock region an unlimited source of color pictures. The towns and villages of Peterborough, Dublin, Jaffrey, Hancock, Francestown—to mention a few—convey New England in most peaceful settings.

Exposure—1/100 of a second at f:14. ASA Speed 50.

ARTHUR GRIFFIN

Perpetual Morning

There are days which occur in this climate, at almost any season of the year, wherein the world reaches its perfection; when the air, the heavenly bodies and the earth, make a harmony, as if nature would indulge her offspring; when, in these bleak upper sides of the planet, nothing is to desire that we have heard of the happiest latitudes, and we bask in the shining hours of Florida and Cuba; when everything that has life gives sign of satisfaction, and the cattle that lie on the ground seem to have great and tranquil thoughts. These halcyons may be looked for with a little more assurance in that pure October weather which we distinguish by the name of the Indian summer. The day, immeasurably long, sleeps over the broad hills and warm wide fields. To have lived through all its sunny hours, seems longevity enough. The solitary places do not seem quite lonely. At the gates of the forest, the surprised man of the world is forced to leave his city estimates of great and small, wise and foolish. The knapsack of custom falls off his back with the first step he takes into these precincts. Here is sanctity which shames our religions, and reality which discredits our heroes. Here we find Nature to be the circumstance which dwarfs every other circumstance, and judges like a god all men that come to her. We have crept out of our close and crowded houses into the night and morning, and we see what majestic beauties daily wrap us in their bosom. How willingly we would escape the barriers which render them comparatively impotent, escape the sophistication and second thought, and suffer nature to intrance us. The tempered light of the woods is like a perpetual morning, and is stimulating and heroic. The anciently-reported spells of these places creep on us. The stems of pines, hemlocks and oaks almost gleam like iron on the excited eye. The incommunicable trees begin to persuade us to live with them, and quit our life of solemn trifles. Here no history, or church, or state, is interpolated on the divine sky and the immortal year. How easily we might walk onward into the opening landscape, absorbed by new pictures and by thoughts fast succeeding each other, until by degrees the recollection of home was crowded out of the mind, all memory obliterated by the tyranny of the present, and we were led in triumph by nature.

RALPH WALDO EMERSON

Emerson, of course, makes an allusion here to Indian Summer, while the world into which we are walking is at the spring. Emerson, however, was a mosaic writer: and should the mosaics be carefully examined, he will often appear to be writing in chords. He makes harmony at any season: distant harmony. He is not poking his head out of Henry Thoreau's cabin. There is no rain on his face. He was not one to have acquired, as Thomas Hardy once reported of someone else, the knack of knowing where he was at night by the particular sound of the wind in particular leaves of the trees. Different leaves on the same trees (the large and small) do make different sounds. Yet Emerson could, in his own way, exalt as well as exult. "Nature" is still one of the greatest of his essays, slice it as you will. And, last of all, I do not normally think of Emerson in Vermont; but if you climb or drive up Mount Mansfield you will find there, under glass, at least one written souvenir of his passing. He got around much more than did Henry. With half a chance, he might have walked to Oregon, always Henry's subconscious destination.

EAST RUPERT, VERMONT

Driving along I saw these clouds building up. I climbed a small hill and waited for some sunlight. It illuminated the foreground briefly, and then was gone. The mountain in the background is Netop (3020 feet). The town of Dorset lies two miles down the road and is a center for the arts. The terraced valley, enclosed by forested marble mountains, makes an ideal setting for such a colony. The writers and artists live here year round. The valley, on route 30, between Manchester and Pawlett, offers wonderful photographic studies. Don't miss the Old Quarry Swimming Pool for pictures, or a swim. Surrounding this very deep, cold pool are enormous chunks of marble which invite interesting studies.

Exposure—1/25 of a second at f:16. ASA Speed 50.

34

ARTHUR GRIFFIN

ARTHUR GRIFFIN

Art Class

The United States was long isolationist in art as in politics. We were preoccupied with developing a vast continent. We took little note of the currents and counter-currents, the ferment in European art. In cityscape pictures the natural bent of our artists in the Nineteenth Century was to depict in a traditional realist American mode, the varied, teeming life of the melting pot. The landscape painters were frankly lyric, sentimental and romantic.

A change took place in the 90's due to the widely acclaimed painting of Whistler and Sargent even though they were both such confirmed expatriates that they were more at home in England than in their native land.

James Abbott McNeill Whistler (1834–1903) learned the etcher's technique making maps for the United States Coast Survey. As etcher he was compared, by American collectors at least, to Rembrandt and Goya:—an overstatement that, even after all these years, is annoying. . . .

Whistler went abroad to paint. On reaching Paris, he was influenced by Courbet and Manet. He was admired by Degas and Fantin-Latour. In London he crossed swords with Ruskin, which led to the famous law suit. Whistler was a caustic critic, a prince of aesthetes, a reckless, irritating wit, an all-round stormy petrel, and a lover of Japanese objects. . .

In the most fundamental sense his interests make him an American ancestor of modern art. The great public uninfluenced by changing fashion and theories is still hypnotized by his name. Quite rightly they acclaim his Louvre masterpiece which Whistler called (significantly from a modern point of view) *Arrangement in Black and Grey*. Actually it is a portrait of his mother. It was acquired for $800 by the French Government after going about unwanted for many years. But four decades later, one of the most popular pictures in the world, it was valued at a half-million dollars.

John Singer Sargent (1856–1925) was, like Whistler, an expatriate. He was a fashionable, unimaginative painter. He was not at his best in his academic portraits in oil nor in his overrated Boston and Cambridge murals. But his watercolors and his early pencil portraits show evidence of his great gift and enormous facility.

Winslow Homer (1836–1910) was a Yankee of seafaring ancestry. Like Eakins, the sober realist, and Ryder, the visionary, Homer was untouched by French Impressionism although he went to the International Exhibition in Paris in 1867. Homer's realism was American. He never lost interest in form. Critics and public alike take pride in his achievement. Never in eclipse, he is today acclaimed as an American dramatic realist. His works are accorded respect and admiration because of his powerful directness of vision . . . because of the technical skill and the love with which man and nature are joined in convincing unity.

Homer's long apprenticeship started in Civil War days as a faithful recorder of camp life. Through woodcuts and engravings of soldiers or of Negroes, of school scenes or of children at play, his honest drawings were reproduced in popular magazines like *Harper's Weekly*. Such commissions strengthened his inborn capacity as a draughtsman. They prepared him for his subsequent technical accomplishments in watercolor, as in oil. . . . Late in life he voiced a prophecy that has come true:—"You will see in the future I will live by my watercolors."

PAUL J. SACHS

The late Paul J. Sachs, when he died in 1965, was Professor of Fine Arts *Emeritus* and Director *Emeritus* of the Fogg Art Museum in Harvard University. The quoted paragraphs from *Modern Prints & Drawings* (the United States) should perhaps have been concluded by his note on still another painter. "*Thomas Eakins* (1844–1916), whose name we bracket with that of Homer, was acclaimed only after his death as one of our great American realists. The two artists were very different in outlook, practice, and training. Eakins, a powerful, conservative portrait painter of rare distinction, took for his subjects the serious people in his immediate milieu. Always an artist of probity, he was austere and cerebral. He was interested in perspective, anatomy, and scientific truth . . . Homer worked out of doors. Eakins, whether indoors or out, collected his data and then with deliberation brought his meticulous paintings to completion in his studio."

This sketching class in Providence, Rhode Island, an artistic arrangement in itself, may or may not contain a future Homer or Eakins (male or female). It is not likely to contain another irrepressible the equal of Whistler. But yet within the covers of *The Gentle Art of Making Enemies*, we strand upon so calm and reflective a passage as the following—reminding us again that Whistler once said, "All great art is low in tone."

"And the evening mist clothes the riverside with poetry, as with a veil, and the poor buildings lose themselves in the dim sky, and the tall chimneys become campanili, and the warehouses are palaces in the night, and the whole city hangs in the heavens, and fairy-land is before us—then the wayfarer hastens home; the working man and the cultured one, the wise man and the one of pleasure, cease to understand, as they have ceased to see, and Nature, who, for once, has sung in tune, sings her exquisite song to the artist alone, her son and her master—her son in that he loves her, and her master in that he knows her."

James Abbott McNeill Whistler

ROGER WILLIAMS PARK, PROVIDENCE, RHODE ISLAND

This park is known throughout the country for its flower gardens and the beauty of its settings. The park contains almost 500 acres, 140 of which are lakes and lagoons. This particular spot, only a few miles from the center of Providence, has beautiful spring flowering trees and flowers. In addition to the floral displays there are a zoo, an aviary and a deer park. On a spring morning I shot just the tree in flat light. That afternoon I returned and found the children with side lighting, which brought out the color of the flowering tree.

Exposure—1/25 of a second at f:22. ASA Speed 50.

ARTHUR GRIFFIN

Parade of the Living

Part of the frailty of man is to see all natural phenomena in the light of his own sensibilities. But even by human standards the laws that govern the phenomena are not invariably cruel. Even in the relationships of creatures to one another there is balm for the tenderminded. In the lush fullness of her harlotry, Nature embraces many things. She embraces love as well as hunger, the love of mate for mate and of mates for offspring. She embraces cooperation as well as conflict, conjugal in the nest and communal in the herd. She embraces loyalty as well as treason, loyalty of individuals to their generation and of generations to their race. She does all this in the self-conscious sight of man. What she does in the sight of the Absolute is less easy to say.

One thing, however, is clear. Just as there have been but few fundamentally different plots in the history of drama so also have there been but few fundamentally different roles. In the drama of life the sun is the protagonist without which there could be no action. Next in importance are the green plants which alone are able to shape the sun's energy to the purposes of the play, and the colorless plants, especially the bacteria, which help keep the plot a-boiling. Then there are the herbivorous animals that eat the plants, the carnivores that eat the herbivores, the saprophytes and scavengers that eat the remains of both. Though countless minor roles have from time to time been added, these are the only invariable and important ones.

JOHN HODGDON BRADLEY

Out of Vermont came a little book ostensibly for younger readers called *Justin Morgan Had a Horse*. In the following passage are the closing lines, which concludes the story, you can see why Vermont is proud of its Morgan strain.

The story of Justin Morgan has not ended. The brave little horse lives on. He had many colts. Six or twelve, or fourteen. Maybe more.

His children, too, had many children. This in itself is not remarkable. But it was exceedingly remarkable that all of the grandchildren should look like Justin Morgan. Carbon copies one might say. They all had the wonderfully proud heads with that wide space between the eyes. They all had the same round-barreled bodies and the short, sturdy legs. And they all had deep chests with ample room for powerful lungs and the Morgan heart. What is more, they all traveled with the same easy grace. Even when they were little foals, it was plain to see that Justin Morgan was the image from which they were made.

The likeness did not stop with looks. It went deeper. Justin Morgan's grandchildren inherited an inner something. Men gave it various names. Courage. Power. Intelligence. The heart to go on forever. Some called it a high free spirit and let it go at that. One driver who carried the mail before the days of the railroad said, "Through blinding sleet and heavy drifts, I never had a Morgan horse look back to refuse me. They always faced the blast. If a double trip had to be made, the Morgans were the ones to do it."

No less than forty descendants of Justin Morgan became famous as trotters. Ethan Allen, Black Hawk, and Cock of the Rock made trotting history. And Dan Patch, who inherited strong Morgan characteristics, set the mile record for pacing, a record which stood for thirty-three years.

Morgans also became the war horses of America. General Custer rode a Morgan horse when he went off to fight the Indians. And in the War Between the States a whole regiment was mounted on Morgans. "It was your *horses* licked us!" a southerner admitted. One of these horses, Rienzi, was ridden by General Sheridan when he hastened to defend the city of Washington. And the ride has gone down in history:

> "Here is the steed that saved the day
> By carrying Sheridan into the fight
> From Winchester, twenty miles away!"

> *(Marguerite Henry)*

WEYBRIDGE, VERMONT

In 1791, a schoolmaster, Justin Morgan, brought to Vermont a colt of such exceptional qualities that it sired a new breed. The breed became famous as the Morgan horse. Within fifty years Morgan horses were found in nearly every state in the union. The State University owns the Morgan Horse Farm (outside of Middlebury) and welcomes tourists. I don't know of a better location for horse photographs, especially in the early spring. I hand-held my roll film camera for this picture.

Exposure—1/200 of a second at f:8. ASA Speed 50.

42

ARTHUR GRIFFIN

Walking with Thoreau

I think I know four kinds of cornel beside the dogwood and bunchberry. The scarlet of the dogwood is the most conspicuous and interesting of the autumnal colors at present.

I love Nature partly because she is not man, but a retreat from him.

The man I meet with is not often so instructive as the silence he breaks.

When your host shuts his door on you, he incloses you in the dwelling of nature.

I never found the companion that was so companionable as solitude.

Only that day dawns to which we awake.

We live thick and are in each other's way.

A man must find his occasions in himself.

I had three chairs in my house; one for solitude, two for friendship, three for society.

The bluebird carries the sky on his back.

I could easily do without the post-office.

HENRY DAVID THOREAU

The light that plays upon this aphoristic page seems complementary to the dogwood spring which opens opposite. Complementary, also, in that Thoreau speaks of the color of dogwood *in the fall*. Another Thoreauvian note which might have been included, could I have been sure of it—and I wasn't and am not now—is not quite suitable for black road travel: "I turn to my solitary woodland walk as the homesick turn home." Robert Frost in the documentary film made shortly before he died says "Me for the woods!" Everybody knows the part that those meticulous journals played in Thoreau's life.

One passes easily from the journals of Emerson to those of Thoreau. The fragmentation is often not dissimilar: in part no doubt because topography, where it occurs with significance for the idea expressed, is likely to be common ground—common mountain, common fields, common river, common sky. "The sky is the daily bread of the eyes" sounds like Thoreau, but it was Emerson who said it. Hawthorne's journals are more like cameos: snatches of biography, background paragraphs, sketches for a scene. It is the difference between the novelist and the philosopher-essayist, the philosopher-naturalist. The current in Hawthorne's journals does not run so deep as in Emerson's or Thoreau's; the flashes of insight are not so dazzling, phrases not so memorable. Of the trinity, the journals which do *not* figure in *Bartlett* are Hawthorne's. But Van Wyck Brooks, for one, saw their importance. The following passage, however, does injustice to the full cavern-image of the human heart, and so I append what Hawthorne himself said in conclusion.

Opening his note-book in the evening, he jotted down his observations. . . . To Hawthorne they were anything but trifling. Every one of these notes possessed for him a golden aureole of associations. Traits of New England life, aspects of New England scenery: a stone wall covered with vines and shrubs and elm-trees that had thrust their roots beneath it, a valley like a vast bowl, filled with yellow sunlight as with wine, the effect of the morning sun on dewy grass, sunlight on a sloping, swelling landscape beyond a river in the middle distance, an afternoon light on a clump of trees, evening light falling on a lonely figure, perhaps a country doctor on his horse. . . Dark trees, decaying stumps, a cave in the side of a hill, with the sunlight playing over it. How like the human heart, this cave, with the glancing sun and the flowers about its entrance! One stepped within and found oneself surrounded with a terrible gloom and monsters of divers kinds.

(Van Wyck Brooks)

You are bewildered, and wander long without hope. At last, a light strikes upon you. You press towards it, and find yourself in a region that seems, in some sort, to reproduce the flowers and sunny beauty of the entrance—but all perfect. These are the depths of the heart, or of human nature, bright and beautiful; the gloom and terror may lie deep, but deeper still is this eternal beauty.

(Nathaniel Hawthorne)

46

GREENFIELD HILL, CONNECTICUT

Each season has a special flavor of its own in Connecticut. I like spring best. Then the woodlands are bright with flowering dogwood and mountain laurel. The spring morning I first drove up to Greenfield Hill, only three miles from Fairfield, I could hardly believe my eyes. The village streets were unbelievably beautiful avenues of pink and white dogwood in full blossom. Not just a few streets. The entire area was a fairyland of bloom. I've been down South many times and have seen their spectacular displays, but none of them can equal this small section of Connecticut for natural flowering color.

Exposure—1/25 of a second at f:20. ASA Speed 50.

ARTHUR GRIFFIN

Baedeker on Provincetown

From Boston to Provincetown
Cape Cod
Comp. Map, p. 232

120 M. Old Colony System of N.Y., N.H. & H. R.R.
(*South Union Station*) in $4\frac{1}{4}$ hrs. (fare $2.40)—
Steamers also ply daily to Provincetown in summer
from *Battery Wharf* (50 M., in 4 hrs; return-fare $1)

• • • • •

120 M. Provincetown (*Central Ho.*, 2\frac{1}{2}$; *Gifford Ho.*,
Pilgrim Ho., $2) is a quaint old fishing-town (cod
and mackerel) with (1905) 4362 inhab. and a fine
land-locked harbour formed by the final crook of
Cape Cod. The town-crier is still an institution
here. The *Mayflower* anchored here on Nov. 11th, 1620,
and this event is commemorated by a monument (1908) on
Town or *High Pole Hill* (good view), modelled (somewhat
strangely) on the tower of the Palazzo Pubblico at
Siena. There is a lighthouse on *Race Point*.

BAEDEKER'S UNITED STATES: 1909

I have quoted from Baedeker not because he is quaint but because he is fiercely objective, and most of our quotations are the opposite of that. He does use the word *quaint* in describing Provincetown, though it is hell-bent quainter today, under an intravenous injection of the tourist antibody, than it ever was in 1909. Note what Baedeker says about the Monument.

His guidebooks are *his* monument. Who was Karl Baedeker? I do not know precisely, familiar as I once was—or thought I was—with some of his many books. If there is a life of him in print, I am and wish to remain unaware of it. Reading it now would be like seeing a movie of a once-loved novel. The man who made the cunning and incredible brief study of him is W. G. Constable: "Three Stars for Baedeker," *Harper's Magazine* for April, 1953. He was, says Mr. Constable—I am cruelly condensing —"a man of great vigor and considerable endurance . . . a great believer in woolen underclothing, 'strong and well-tried boots.'" He carried "besides a light waterproof and a stout umbrella, an opera glass or small telescope, sewing materials, a supply of strong cord, sticking plaster, a small compass, a pocket lantern, a thermometer, and an aneroid barometer . . . He was encyclopedic rather than learned, informative rather than inspiring. . . ." He always preferred rooms with a southern exposure, warned all his readers against unripe fruit, macaroni, and fish, and "carried with him a copious supply of remedies, more or less drastic." I don't know how he made out at Provincetown. He must somehow have countered the question of fish. I strongly doubt that a pizzi had reached the Cape that early.

50

PROVINCETOWN, MASSACHUSETTS

Here where Cape Cod goes down to the sea, nestles Provincetown, the best known (before Hyannisport became famous) and the most picturesque of its old villages. It was the first landing place of the Pilgrims, a center of whaling, an important fishing port, and now the location of a famous art colony. Almost surrounded by sea, Provincetown is some 120 miles over the road from Boston, but only 40 miles by sea. I could write about the good old days of P-Town with Nostalgia, vintage of '25, but why? You can still find plenty of wonderful pictures if you are as lucky as I was the day I made this late afternoon study five years ago. Then you could drive down on the pier where these boats were docked. From Commercial Street (the main drag) we saw the late stormy sun starting to strike the fishing fleet, hurried down and just got this and another picture before the sun went down behind us.

Exposure—1/25 of a second at f:16. ASA Speed 50.

ARTHUR GRIFFIN

Longfellow Country

One Autumn night, in Sudbury town,
Across the meadows bare and brown,
The windows of the wayside inn
Gleamed red with fire-light through the leaves
Of woodbine, hanging from the eaves
Their crimson curtains rent and thin.

As ancient is this hostelry
As any in the land may be,
Built in the old Colonial day,
When men lived in a grander way,
With ampler hospitality;
A kind of old Hobgoblin Hall,
Now somewhat fallen to decay,
With weather-stains upon the wall,
And stairways worn, and crazy doors,
And creaking and uneven floors,
And chimneys huge, and tiled and tall.

A region of repose it seems,
A place of slumber and of dreams,
Remote among the wooded hills!
For there no noisy railway speeds,
Its torch-race scattering smoke and gleeds;

But noon and night, the panting teams
Stop under the great oaks, that throw
Tangles of light and shade below,
On roofs and doors and window-sills.
Across the road the barns display
Their lines of stalls, their mows of hay,
Through the wide doors the breezes blow,
The wattled cocks strut to and fro,
And, half effaced by rain and shine,
The Red Horse prances on the sign.

Round this old-fashioned, quaint abode
Deep silence reigned, save when a gust
Went rushing down the country road,
And skeletons of leaves, and dust,
A moment quickened by its breath,
Shuddered and danced their dance of death,
And through the ancient oaks o'erhead
Mysterious voices moaned and fled.

HENRY WADSWORTH LONGFELLOW

53

These opening lines (the Prelude) of *Tales of a Wayside Inn* continue:

> But from the parlor of the inn
> A pleasant murmur smote the ear,
> Like water rushing through a weir . . .

And why not, with the now famous grist mill just across the post road? The mill dates from 1929; and the Inn from about 1686. Why not, indeed! Henry Ford gave us this working replica. But we tend to forget that grist mills, quaint and curious as they now seem to us in restoration, were almost as common a sight centuries ago as Red Coach Grills today, always considering the far smaller population and generally restricted travel, even on a post road.

Who reads *Tales of a Wayside Inn* today? More people in England than here, most likely. It runs to eighty-four two-column pages of seven-point type that reads like six in my household edition. Consider that you have read it: all the tales of all that firelight company: Landlord, Student, Young Sicilian, Spanish Jew, Theologian, Poet, Musician—and not least the Landlord's "Paul Revere's Ride"—then here is the ending.

> "Farewell!" the portly Landlord cried;
> "Farewell!" the parting guest replied,
> But little thought that nevermore
> Their feet would pass that threshold o'er;
> That nevermore together there
> Would they assemble, free from care,
> To hear the oaks' mysterious roar,
> And breathe the wholesome country air.
>
> Where are they now? What lands and skies
> Paint pictures in their friendly eyes?
> What hope deludes, what promise cheers,
> What pleasant voices fill their ears?
> Two are beyond the salt sea waves,
> And three already in their graves.
> Perchance the living still may look
> Into the pages of this book,
> And see the days of long ago
> Floating and fleeting to and fro,
> As in the well-remembered brook
> They saw the inverted landscape gleam,
> And their own faces like a dream
> Look up upon them from below.
> (Henry Wadsworth Longfellow)

SUDBURY, MASSACHUSETTS

Camera fans have at least three wonderful subjects here. Henry Ford built this mill in 1929 and restored the Wayside Inn, immortalized by Longfellow in "Tales of a Wayside Inn," and he built the Martha Mary Chapel in memory of his mother and his wife's mother. Next to the Chapel, set in a grove of pines, is the small red schoolhouse. A tablet on a huge boulder near it notes that the school is the one made famous in the poem "Mary Had a Little Lamb."

I almost used a picture of the Wayside Inn for this scene, but this grist mill, surely the most photogenic in New England, is as representative both of the area, and of "Tales of a Wayside Inn." Fire swept the old Wayside Inn three nights before Christmas a decade ago. I rushed out early the next morning and captured some wonderful pictures of the Inn and trees covered with ice. The Ford Foundation with a grant of half-a-million came to the rescue, and it is now closer to the original Inn when Washington and Lafayette slept there. The dormers and other unsympathetic additions which were added through the years were removed, and as the interior was not damaged to great extent, these founders of our nation (could they but return!) might notice only the prices and that the waitresses are prettier.

Exposure—1/25 of a second at f:16. ASA Speed 50.

ARTHUR GRIFFIN

North of Kipling

Followed, Summer, angry, fidgety, and nervous, with the corn and tobacco to ripen in five short months, the pastures to reclothe, and the fallen leaves to hide away under new carpets. Suddenly, in the middle of her work, on a stuffy-still July day, she called a wind out of the Northwest, a wind blown under an arch of steel-bellied clouds, a wicked bitter wind with a lacing of hail to it, a wind that came and was gone in less than ten minutes, but blocked the roads with fallen trees, toppled over a barn, and—blew potatoes out of the ground! When that was done, a white cloud shaped like a dumb-bell whirled down the valley across the evening blue, roaring and twisting and twisting and roaring all alone by itself. A West Indian hurricane could not have been quicker on its feet than our little cyclone, and when the house rose a-tiptoe, like a cockerel in act to crow, and a sixty-foot elm went by the board, and that which had been a dusty road became a roaring torrent all in three minutes, we felt that the New England summer had creole blood in her veins. She went away, red-faced and angry to the last, slamming all the doors of the hills behind her, and Autumn, who is a lady, took charge.

RUDYARD KIPLING

"Reality is Kipling's romanticism," says Louis Untermeyer. I don't recall what T. S. Eliot said in parallel or opposition to that in *A Choice of Kipling's Verse*. Whenever Kipling is damned for his far-flung praise of Empire—but remember how he offended Queen Victoria—he is likely to be damned inadvertently by a phrase which he himself coined. A lot of Kipling is hip and thigh of the English language as we handle or manhandle it. His case is not much different from that of the author of *To Lhasa in Disguise* who, when the Tibetan mob stoned the window of his supposed lodgings, went out and joined it and threw some stones himself. When Kipling married an American in 1892, he settled for a few years in Brattleboro, Vermont. It was there he wrote the *Just-So Stories*, among many other things, and a puckish-cheerful poem called "Pan in Vermont." Who among us has ever caught the fell full splendor of a summer storm in exit equal to those nine words: "slamming all the doors of the hills behind her"? He could write; which is most of what mattered to Eliot and Somerset Maugham—two very different breeds of Angelical cats.

READING, VERMONT

The Jenne farm outside of South Woodstock lends itself to wonderful pictures in all seasons. This farm has been photographed by camera clubs and many other photographers, for it is one of the most picturesque in Vermont. In my other all-color book New England *I showed this same view in fall foliage. The Woodstock area is noted for its trails and dirt roads for horseback riding. The settings are perfect for pictures. Around most any bend in the road you might find that prize study, unspoiled by wires or other eyesores. I like morning light best for this farm.*

Exposure—1/25 of a second at f:18. ASA Speed 50.

ARTHUR GRIFFIN

SUMMER

The Man Against the Sky

Between me and the sunset, like a dome
Against the glory of a world on fire,
Now burned a sudden hill,
Bleak, round, and high, by flame-lit height made higher,
With nothing on it for the flame to kill
Save one who moved and was alone up there
To loom before the chaos and the glare
As if he were the last god going home
Unto his last desire.

Dark, marvelous, and inscrutable he moved on
Till down the fiery distance he was gone,
Like one of those eternal, remote things
That range across a man's imaginings
When a sure music fills him and he knows
What he may say thereafter to few men,—
The touch of ages having wrought
An echo and a glimpse of what he thought
A phantom or a legend until then;
For whether lighted over ways that save,
Or lured from all repose,
If he go on too far to find a grave,
Mostly alone he goes.

Even he, who stood where I had found him,
On high with fire all round him,
Who moved along the molten west,
And over the round hill's crest
That seemed half ready with him to go down,
Flame-bitten and flame-cleft,
As if there were to be no last thing left
Of a nameless unimaginable town,—

Even he who climbed and vanished may have taken
Down to the perils of a depth not known,
From death defended though by men forsaken,
The bread that every man must eat alone;
He may have walked while others hardly dared
Look on to see him stand where many fell;
And upward out of that, as out of hell,
He may have sung and striven
To mount where more of him shall yet be given,
Bereft of all retreat,
To sevenfold heat,—
As on a day when three in Dura shared
The furnace, and were spared
For glory by that king of Babylon
Who made himself so great that God, who heard,
Covered him with long feathers, like a bird.

EDWIN ARLINGTON ROBINSON

Sunset flares at some point in almost every poet. We sail beyond it with Ulysses or we linger as did Edwin Arlington Robinson. He lingered best in one poem to which he gave a title as splendid as the bold dynamic lines which follow it; and if you have not lately read "The Man Against the Sky," at least you have read or reread the opening forty-six lines of one of the lasting American poems of this century. It is impossible for me to watch a sunset—*crescit eundo*—over Lake Champlain or from Campobello over Eastport, without thinking of it.

It was President Franklin D. Roosevelt who summered at the site of Arthur Griffin's camera-study setting; but it was President Theodore Roosevelt who befriended the impoverished Robinson with a clerkship in the New York Custom House (1905–1910) ten years or so before "The Man Against the Sky" was written.

SUNSET FROM CAMPOBELLO

The sun was setting over Eastport, Maine, and the site of the proposed Passamaquoddy Tidal Power Project. I just managed to get this shot before the thickest cloud of gnats and mosquitoes I have ever seen almost devoured both the camera and me. This picture is from the beach in front of the summer home of the late President Franklin D. Roosevelt. The sunsets from this shore can be really fabulous. The fishing weir in the foreground is common in Canadian waters and offers interesting camera studies; the famed 30-foot Bay of Fundy tides provide constant changes of composition. You reach Campobello Island over a new bridge from Lubec. This island has photogenic villages and magnificent panoramic views of the sea and the Maine coast.

Exposure—1/25 of a second at f:11. ASA Speed 50.

Steady as You Go

"No, Stubb; you may pound that knot there as much as you please, but you will never pound into me what you were just now saying. And how long ago is it since you said the very contrary? Didn't you once say that whatever ship Ahab sails in, that ship should pay something extra on its insurance policy, just as though it were loaded with powder barrels aft and boxes of lucifers forward? Stop, now; didn't you say so?"

"Well, suppose I did? What then? I've part changed my flesh since that time, why not my mind? Besides, supposing we *are* loaded with powder barrels aft and lucifers forward; how the devil could the lucifers get afire in this drenching spray here? Why, my little man, you have pretty red hair, but you couldn't get afire now. Shake yourself; you're Aquarius, or the waterbearer, Flask; might fill pitchers at your coat collar. Don't you see, then, that for these extra risks the Marine Insurance companies have extra guarantees? . . . What's the might difference between holding a mast's lightning-rod in the storm, and standing close by a mast that hasn't got any lightning-rod at all in a storm? Don't you see, you timber-head, that no harm can come to the holder of the rod, unless the mast is first struck? What are you talking about, then? Not one ship in a hundred carries rods, and Ahab,—aye, man, and all of us,—were in no more danger then, in my poor opinion, than all the crews in ten thousand ships now sailing the seas. Why, you King-Post, you, I suppose you would have every man in the world go about with a small lightning-rod running up the corner of his hat, like a militia officer's skewered feather, and trailing behind like his sash. Why don't ye be sensible, Flask? it's easy to be sensible; why don't ye, then? any man with half an eye can be sensible."

"I don't know that, Stubb. You sometimes find it rather hard."

"Yes, when a fellow's soaked through, it's hard to be sensible, that's a fact. And I am about drenched with this spray. Never mind; catch the turn there, and pass it. Seems to me we are lashing down these anchors now as if they were never going to be used again. . . . I wonder, Flask, whether the world is anchored anywhere; if she is, she swings with an uncommon long cable, though. There, hammer that knot down, and we've done. So; next to touching land, lighting on deck is the most satisfactory. I say, just wring out my jacket skirts, will ye? Thank ye. They laugh at long-togs so, Flask; but seems to me, a long tailed coat ought always to be worn in all storms afloat. The tails tapering down that way, serve to carry off the water, d'ye see. Same with cocked hats; the cocks form gable-end eave-troughs, Flask. No more monkey-jackets and tarpaulins for me; I must mount a swallow-tail, and drive down a beaver; so. Halloa! whew! there goes my tarpaulin overboard; Lord, Lord, that the winds that come from heaven should be so unmannerly! This is a nasty night, lad."

HERMAN MELVILLE

What could one say, I thought, about this huddle of hulls lapsing into fog, uneasy as a rudder in the long stretch before Bermuda landfall? A yachting piece would be too special for the land-lubber; certainly for me. Something out of *The Riddle in the Sands*: that would be it. But Erskine Childers and the North Sea will not satisfy the equation of a New England book. Nor is Newport yet New Bedford; but the ghost of Ahab never fades too far astern on any cruise, hence my choice of Stubb and Flask. Much as I lean toward Queequeg, I always had a strong affection for Stubb: for "when Stubb dressed, instead of first putting his legs into his trousers, he put his pipe into his mouth."

Another choice for this Newport berth was Anthony Trollope who visited there in 1861 and likely saw this very point of land.

There is excellent bathing [said Trollope] for those who like bathing on shelving sand. I don't. The spot is about half a mile from the hotels, and to this the bathers are carried in omnibuses. Till one o'clock ladies bathe;—which operation, however, does not at all militate against the bathing of men, but rather necessitates it as regards those men who have ladies with them. For here ladies and gentlemen bathe in decorous dresses, and are very polite to each other. I must say, that I think the ladies have the best of it. My idea of sea-bathing for my own gratification is not compatible with the full suit of clothing. I own that my tastes are vulgar and perhaps indecent; but I love to jump into the deep clear sea from off a rock, and I love to be hampered by no outward impediments as I do so. For ordinary bathers, for all ladies, and for men less savage in their instincts than I am, the bathing at Newport is very good.

(*Anthony Trollope*)

68

START OF NEWPORT-BERMUDA RACE, NEWPORT, RHODE ISLAND

This is a bi-annual event off Newport, and I was very disappointed (everyone else was, too) with the heavy fog. I made this from the upper deck of the Coast Guard vessel, right at the starting line. It certainly was the ideal place to be with all those beautiful yachts milling around, waiting for the gun. Frankly, I was surprised how well this came out. In some of my pictures the Ektachrome film seemed to penetrate the fog. I hand-held my roll-film camera for this picture.

Exposure—1/100 of a second at f:16. ASA Speed 50.

ARTHUR GRIFFIN

The Shet-up Posy

But one day, afore she'd got very old, 'fore she'd dried up or fell off, or anything like that, she see somebody comin' along her way. 'Twas a man, and he was lookin' at all the posies real hard and partic'lar, but he wasn't pickin' any of 'em. Seems 's if he was lookin' for somethin' diff'rent from what he see, and the poor little shet-up posy begun to wonder what he was arter. Bimeby she braced up, and she asked him about it in her shet-up, whisp'rin' voice. And says he, the man says: "I'm a-pickin' posies. That's what I work at most o' the time. 'Tain't for myself," he says, "but the one I work for. I'm on'y his help. I run errands and do chores for him, and it's a partic'lar kind o' posy he's sent me for to-day." "What for does he want 'em?" says the shet-up posy. "Why, to set out in his gardin," the man says. "He's got the beautif'lest gardin you never see, and I pick posies for 't." "Deary me," thinks she to herself, "I jest wish he'd pick me. But I ain't the kind, I know." And then she says, so soft he can't hardly hear her, "What sort o' posies is it you're arter this time?" "Well," says the man, "it's a dreadful sing'lar order I've got to-day. I got to find a posy that's handsomer inside than 'tis outside, one that folks ain't took no notice of here, 'cause 'twas kind o' humly and queer to look at, not knowin' that inside 'twas as handsome as any posy on the airth. Seen any o' that kind?" says the man.

Well, the shet-up posy was dreadful worked up. "Deary dear!" she says to herself, "now if they'd on'y finished me off inside! I'm the right kind outside, humly and queer enough, but there's nothin' worth lookin' at inside,—I'm certin sure o' that." But she didn't say this nor anything else out loud, and bimeby, when the man had waited, and didn't get any answer, he begun to look at the shet-up posy more partic'lar, to see why she was so mum. And all of a suddent he says, the man did, "Looks to me 's if you was somethin' that kind yourself, ain't ye?" "Oh, no, no, no!" whispers the shet-up posy. "I wish I was, I wish I was. I'm all right outside, humly and awk'ard, queer's I can be, but I ain't pretty inside,—oh! I most know I ain't." "I ain't so sure o' that myself," says the man, "but I can tell in a jiffy." "Will you have to pick me to pieces?" says the shet-up posy. "No, ma'am," says the man; "I've got a way o' tellin', the one I work for showed me." The shet-up posy never knowed what he done to her. I don't know myself, but 'twas somethin' soft and pleasant, that didn't hurt a mite, and then the man he says, "Well, well, well." That's all he said, but he took her up real gentle, and begun to carry her away. "Where be ye takin' me?" says the shet-up posy. "Where ye belong," says the man; "to the gardin o' the one I work for," he says. "I didn't know I was nice enough inside," says the shet-up posy, very soft and still. "They most gen'-ally don't," says the man.

ANNIE TRUMBULL SLOSSON

Annie Trumbull Slosson, born in Stonington, Connecticut (see page 105), is almost forgotten today. She never shouted. Her tiny voice is like the small shet-up posy in the story of that name from which the previous paragraphs are taken. But those who have read her have not forgotten that at least one story—"The Boy Who Was Scaret o'Dyin'"—is a classic of its kind; a favorite forty years ago with Charles Townsend Copeland of Harvard. Stephen Vincent Benét never heard Copey read it aloud, but it had one pin-point moment of influence on "The Devil and Daniel Webster". Find it, read it, then read or reread Benét, and you will see almost instantly just where.

Another passage which alone would sustain this flowery glimpse of Perkins Cove is by Sarah Orne Jewett. Even so, it makes a fine companion piece for that of A. T. S.

There are few of us who cannot remember a front-yard garden which seemed to us a very paradise in childhood. It was like a miracle when the yellow and white daffies came into bloom in the spring, and there was a time when tiger-lilies and the taller rose-bushes were taller than we were, and we could not look over their heads as we do now. There were always a good many lady's-delights that grew under the bushes, and came up anywhere in the chinks of the walk or the door-step, and there was a little green sprig called ambrosia that was a famous stray-away. Outside the fence one was not unlikely to see a company of French pinks, which were forbidden standing-room inside as if they were tiresome poor relations of the other flowers. I always felt a sympathy for French pinks,—they have a fresh, sweet look, as if they resigned themselves to their lot in life and made the best of it, and remembered that they had the sunshine and rain, and could see what was going on in the world, if they were outlaws.

I like to remember being sent on errands, and being asked to wait while the mistress of the house picked some flowers to send back to my mother. They were almost always prim, flat bouquets in those days; the larger flowers were picked first and stood at the back and looked over the heads of those that were shorter of stem and stature, and the givers always sent a message that they had not stopped to arrange them. I remember that I had even then a great dislike to lemon verbena, and that I would have waited patiently outside a gate all the afternoon if I knew that some one would kindly give me a sprig of lavender in the evening. And lilies did not seem to me overdressed, but it was easy for me to believe that Solomon in all his glory was not arrayed like a great yellow marigold, or even the dear little single ones that were yellow and brown, and bloomed until the snow came.

(Sarah Orne Jewett)

PERKINS COVE, OGUNQUIT, MAINE

Too often photographers in the East can see only the grandeur of the mountains and seashore, when the greatest beauty can be right at their feet, so to speak. I always look for something to frame a picture, and these flowers did just that. This scene was made from the garden of one of the many restaurants bordering this interesting small harbor. The village abounds with gift and antique shops, fishing and sport craft, art galleries and art schools. Camera fans can find nearby scores of photogenic subjects at Bald Head Cliffs and Nubble Light, just a stone's-throw from the shore and the hard, smooth beaches.

Exposure—1/10 of a second at f:32. ASA Speed 50.

ARTHUR GRIFFIN

Gay Head

The Indians appear to have had two fabulous giants or devils, Cheepii and Moshop. Not much has been handed down concerning the former; [but it seems] probable that the original Moshop was a real Indian, a man of parts who left his impress, and about whose memory was gradually collected the legends of the region. The following legend tells how he was outwitted and his work brought to naught by the cunning of an old woman. Those living on the Vineyard wished to secure easy access to the island of Cuttyhunk, and begged Moshop to build a bridge across, while the Cuttyhunkers, who were satisfied with their home trade, and desired not the intrusion of foreigners, as earnestly begged him not to build; thus was he torn between two opinions, until finally his home friends prevailed and he consented, the only stipulation being that he was to begin at sunset and stop at cockcrow, whether the bridge was finished or not. This, however, would give ample time.

Then were they of Cuttyhunk much alarmed and exercised, being wholly unable to devise any means to stay his hand until an old woman came forward and said that if watch was kept and she informed when Moshop began, she would stop him. Her friends thought her crazy, asking how a poor, weak woman could stop such a great giant, when the strength of all the men of Cuttyhunk could not prevail against him. But she persisted, and they finally agreed. Thus a sharp watch was kept every sunset until finally Moshop was seen to approach the shore with a great rock in his hands and, as the sun took his evening dip in the western waters, to throw it far out into the Sound.

Then came rocks in a shower, some as large as the greatest wigwams, and the bridge began rapidly to grow. All Cuttyhunk was soon on the beach, watching by the dying light of day the terrific pace at which Moshop worked, and it was only when it became too dark to see that they bethought them of the old woman and ran to her with cries and taunts, asking what she was going to do about it, but she dismissed them to their homes. Then went she in unto her cock, and passing a bright light before his eyes caused him to awake with the thought of dawn in his mind, whereupon he lustily began to crow and Moshop was, by the bargain he had made, compelled to stop his work. But the rocks remain even unto this day, and many a good ship has gone to pieces on the Devil's Bridge.

C. G. HINE

The tale of New England's Paul Bunyan comes from *Martha's Vineyard*, collected and arranged by C. G. Hine. As to the geology of this stunning headland, here is a description by Nathaniel Southgate Shaler, born in 1841, remembered as a famous and beloved professor of paleontology, then of geology at Harvard (1869–1906):

> Gay Head presents by far the most striking geological features on our eastern shore. . . . These beds contain a greater variety of fossils than can be obtained in any other part of the coast region of New England. . . . A series of great cliffs leading down to the sea; these are of sands and clays having an amazing variety of colors, giving to the whole a brilliancy unexampled except at Alum Bay, Isle of Wight. Red, black, yellow, green and white, with many intermediate tints, are blended in bands which stand nearly vertical on the cliff. Some of the sands abound in sharks' teeth and bones of whales, and in other monuments of another time. Far out to sea we may perceive by the lines of breakers where lie the remnants of the cliffs which have been eaten back for miles. The sands and clays melt in the ravenous waves; the boulders are harder to grind, and remain after the rest has gone.
>
> *(Nathaniel S. Shaler)*

For a note on the botany of Gay Head, Professor Edward Sanford Burgess, sometime of the Hopkins and Hunter College, meets at twilight an old Indian woman (Aunt Biah Diamond) famous for her knowledge of herbs. He has spent the day collecting. She has been beach-plumming ("but it was mostly huckleberries") and starts to tell him about his plants which he is showing her. Professor Burgess was born in 1855 and died in 1928. "Aunt Biah Diamond" reminds one of Myra Buttle, the name that Victor Purcell used to sign *The Sweeniad* in 1957.

> "There's Mayweed (*Anthemis Cotula*); there was none on Gay Head till I set it out; but now it grows well here."
>
> But, said I, why did you care to set it out when it smells so? "Yes, and it tastes just as it smells; but if you steep it and drink it, there's nothing like it for a broken bone; why, it'll almost set a bone itself."
>
> Another little plant which has never acquired a common name of its own among the whites, a stiff bunch of stems with fluffy whitened leaves, *Helianthemum incanum*; "You've Cankerweed", said she, "we gather it to drink for sore mouth; they come here from New Bedford to get it."
>
> I had some Sensitive-fern root, *Onoclea sensibilis*, and it brought out a survival in her daily utterance; of the vanishing word *tush* for tooth.
>
> "Copper-leaf is this next" (speaking of *Pyrola rotundifolia*; the false wintergreen of the books); "very good for a sore, very drawing. It's name? because in winter you'll find the underside of the leaf, it's the color of copper."
>
> *(Edward S. Burgess)*

76

GAY HEAD, MARTHA'S VINEYARD, MASSACHUSETTS

New England offers a wonderful variety of topography along its miles of coastline, and none more colorful than the extraordinary clay cliffs of Gay Head, which is now a National Landmark. Composed of variegated vertical strata of clay ranging from white and blue to orange, red and tan, the precipice, in the rays of the late afternoon sun, presents a gorgeous reflection. From here on a clear day you can see Cape Cod and Rhode Island. In this view on the far horizon is the faint tracery of the Elizabeth Islands over the blue water of Vineyard Sound. From here you can get beautiful sunsets; and twenty miles away, on the eastern end of the island you'll find sunrises without equal. Gay Head is one of the two towns in Massachusetts still mainly occupied by people of Indian descent. Nearby, the harbor of the old fishing village of Menemsha is filled with colorful boats of all types. Afternoon light is best for Gay Head. I used a Polaroid filter to get the depth and color of the water.

Exposure—1/25 of a second at f:10. ASA Speed 50.

Arthur Griffin

Sail On!

Even at this distance I can see the tides,
　　Upheaving, break unheard along its base,
A speechless wrath, that rises and subsides
　　In the white lip and tremor of the face.

And as the evening darkens, lo! how bright,
　　Through the deep purple of the twilight air,
Beams forth the sudden radiance of its light
　　With strange, unearthly splendor in the glare!

The startled waves leap over it; the storm
　　Smites it with all the scourges of the rain,
And steadily against its solid form
　　Press the great shoulders of the hurricane.

The sea-bird wheeling round it, with the din
　　Of wings and winds and solitary cries,
Blinded and maddened by the light within,
　　Dashes himself against the glare, and dies.

A new Prometheus, chained upon the rock,
　　Still grasping in his hand the fire of Jove,
It does not hear the cry, nor heed the shock,
　　But hails the mariner with words of love.

"Sail on!" it says, "sail on, ye stately ships!
　　And with your floating bridge the ocean span:
Be mine to guard this light from all eclipse,
　　Be yours to bring man nearer unto man!"

HENRY WADSWORTH LONGFELLOW

Students of Longfellow will know of what lighthouse he is writing. The notes in my household edition do not say. But while we are Down East, and with such noble sight of water and the Camden Hills, it is not too far a passage through the thoroughfares to Blue Hill and Mary Ellen Chase. In *A Goodly Heritage* she says of her girlhood in the nineties:

We knew and cherished with no little covetousness the stories of the "traders," which had gladdened the hearts of children of an earlier generation. A trader was a vessel from Boston or New York which earned the livelihood of its captain, or perchance of its owner, by carrying annually into the smaller harbours of the coast every kind of ware imaginable and selling its multifarious cargo at prices which the village stores could not meet. Blue Hill children of the sixties and seventies had waited months for the arrival of this floating junk-shop, scanning the sea from every hill and headland for an unfamiliar sail. According to the older people among us, its captain was invariably an accommodating soul, who was not in the least averse to interpreting as coin of the realm any stray bits of old iron, in exchange for which he would proffer oranges and great Boston apples, gorgeously striped candies, dates, figs, and nuts. Moreover, he carried in his hold, for those who had been most thrifty and parsimonious of their small savings, doll buggies and pop-guns, and for the despair of fathers and mothers, who could be lured to the wharf, bolts of cloth and shiny new shoes with voluptuous and alluring tassels. . . . Even we in the nineties knew at first hand something of this sort of supply and demand. When I was in the neighborhood of twelve, my father, together with three other men of the village, bought a quarter share in a two-masted schooner called *The Gold Hunter* . . . [which] brought delighted satisfaction to four large families. *The Gold Hunter* was summarily dispatched to Boston with divers commissions to be accomplished by her relieved captain, and we waited with atavistic feverishness for her return . . . Most remarkable of all her goods in those relatively fruitless days were crates of oranges, two kegs of white grapes, packed in sawdust, and—most wonderful to relate!—a huge bunch of bananas in a long, slatted frame. . . . The acknowledgment of our supremacy over all the other children in town began as soon as the bananas had been lifted from their frame, cleared of their wiry grass, and hung from a beam in our cellar. Visible from the entrance of our bulkhead, they immediately attracted a crowd of spectators. There was hardly a school-less hour, indeed, for a space of three days, when half a dozen pairs of eyes were not gazing in wonder and envy down those stone stairs.

(Mary Ellen Chase)

80

PENOBSCOT BAY FROM VINALHAVEN, MAINE

The coast of Maine is spattered with islands—loads of them. Some are just large enough for a few sea gulls to alight on. Others you can drive to over causeways. Then there are some you can reach by car ferry, such as Vinalhaven from Rockland. All Maine islands have much to offer the artist, photographer or bird watcher. This island is the center of the greatest lobster production in the world. From its quarries was mined granite for government buildings in Washington and the massive columns in the cathedral of St. John the Divine in New York. With Browns Head Light in the foreground, you overlook the blue waters of Penobscot Bay toward the Camden Hills. There's no general washday for a lighthouse housewife, because of heavy fogs. I recall hitting Quoddy Head Light away down east at Lubec on an important rush color assignment. I got the pictures and happened to mention what a beautiful day it was; I was told that the sun came out as I drove down the hill and that the Keeper's wife hadn't been able to hang out her wash for almost a month.

Exposure—1/25 of a second at f:24. ASA Speed 50.

ARTHUR GRIFFIN

Sense of Wonder

A child's world is fresh and new and beautiful, full of wonder and excitement. It is our misfortune that for most of us that clear-eyed vision, that true instinct for what is beautiful and awe-inspiring, is dimmed and even lost before we reach adulthood. If I had influence with the good fairy who is supposed to preside over the christening of all children I should ask that her gift to each child in the world be a sense of wonder so indestructible that it would last throughout life, as an unfailing antidote against the boredom and disenchantments of later years, the sterile preoccupation with things that are artificial, the alienation from the sources of our strength.

If a child is to keep alive his inborn sense of wonder without any such gift from the fairies, he needs the companionship of at least one adult who can share it, rediscovering with him the joy, excitement and mystery of the world we live in. Parents often have a sense of inadequacy when confronted on the one hand with the eager, sensitive mind of a child and on the other with a world of complex physical nature, inhabited by a life so various and unfamiliar that it seems hopeless to reduce it to order and knowledge. In a mood of self-defeat, they exclaim, "How can I possibly teach my child about nature—why, I don't even know one bird from another!"

I sincerely believe that for the child, and for the parent seeking to guide him, it is not half so important to *know* as to *feel*. If facts are the seeds that later produce knowledge and wisdom, then the emotions and the impressions of the senses are the fertile soil in which the seeds must grow. The years of early childhood are the time to prepare the soil. Once the emotions have been aroused—a sense of the beautiful, the excitement of the new and the unknown, a feeling of sympathy, pity, admiration or love—then we wish for knowledge about the object of our emotional response. Once found, it has lasting meaning. It is more important to pave the way for the child to want to know than to put him on a diet of facts he is not ready to assimilate.

RACHEL CARSON

For many children the seashore is the happiest playground they will ever know. Rachel Carson in this present excerpt happens not to mention the sea —and she is first of all a writer of the sea and of the shore and tidal waters—but her posthumous book, *The Sense of Wonder*, is very much a seashore book in which her young nephew, Roger, figures largely. Furthermore, the camera study at which you are looking is not of her familiar Maine but of the National Seashore Park on Cape Cod, not far from Provincetown: not far likewise—a matter of several miles—from the Coast Guard cottage (now a monument) where Henry Beston wrote *The Outermost House*, first published in 1928. So if this strip of sand reminds me of *The Sense of Wonder*, it also reminds me of what Mr. Beston has to say about the mystery of the night sky sown with stars. Here in part is what he wrote nearly forty years ago:

Learn to reverence night and to put away the vulgar fear of it, for, with the banishment of night from the experience of man, there vanishes as well a religious emotion, a poetic mood, which gives depth to the adventure of humanity. By day, space is one with the earth and with man— it is his sun that is shining, his clouds that are floating past; at night, space is his no more. When the great earth, abandoning day, rolls up the deeps of the heavens and the universe, a new door opens for the human spirit, and there are few so clownish that some awareness of the mystery of being does not touch them as they gaze. For a moment of night we have a glimpse of ourselves and of our world islanded in its stream of stars—pilgrims of mortality, voyaging between horizons across the eternal seas of space and time. Fugitive though the instant be, the spirit of man is, during it, ennobled by a genuine moment of emotional dignity, and poetry makes its own both the human spirit and experience.

(Henry Beston)

CAPE COD NATIONAL SEASHORE PARK, MASSACHUSETTS

This area contains some of the most beautiful seashore vistas in America, encompassing some forty miles of clean wide beaches, high sand dunes and at times wonderful surf with rolling waves. The Cape abounds in beaches, only a few miles off heavily traveled route 6. I cannot walk on the outer beach but that I think of Henry Beston. For my previous book he wrote an essay for a picture of the remnants of an old fishing schooner which was wrecked on this beach. In making beach or snow pictures, bear in mind that the light is about double the normal intensity. Therefore stop your lens aperture down one stop or shoot at a higher shutter speed. For this picture I used my roll-film camera hand-held.

Exposure—1/100 of a second at f:16. ASA Speed 50.

ARTHUR GRIFFIN

Architecture of Concentration

Then said I before the hypervian hills and echoes of melancholy, 'Ottaw!' and the door rolled open like a worsted mitten on a woodpile.

Worn with a tumult of the conflict of Hebrew and the scrutiny of salvation, are you consumed with your mountaneous circumstances?

Sakes of life and fountain of all headways, transfrom us by the ornaments of testimonial pardonation to the shadglooms of eternity.

Oh, they are fine. They catch the breezes of hemlock and revolve the pride of education.

Who existed this earth anyway?

Crucifixin' yourself in the observations of life in the gray dawn over your jewelry.

Rimrack the cantaginous rocks of the Berkshire, Greylock, and the Hoosac Tunnel, and build with the architecture of concentration.

May the whale-gates of parmenity transform my elevation and concess my headways of bluce in the ornaments of munition and the tain of gollidge.

Yes, sir, said I, but I won't go into it at night while them cows, snakes, and hydrants are over the doors.

It was dovetailed with silver.

BILL PRATT THE SAW-BUCK PHILOSOPHER

Apart from graduates of Williams College, those who recognize Bill Pratt will likely remember him solely from his brief but memorable appearance in *A Professor of Life* (1923) by Carroll Perry, minister-brother of Bliss Perry of Princeton, the *Atlantic*, and Harvard, and of Lewis Perry of Phillips Exeter Academy. In his brief voiceful day, Alexander Woollcott used the microphone to exalt the genuine—let me add the exceptional—pleasures of this pocket biography of the author's remarkable father. But in 1895 Dr. Perry (Williams '90) and John Sheridan Zelie ('89) had together written a little book called *Bill Pratt The Saw-Buck Philosopher*—"the best-known man Williamstown ever had." Of this rare volume, Talcott Miner Banks (Williams '90) edited a new edition in 1915, adding fresh material—q.v., if your bookseller can nose down a copy. He likely can't. In any event, you have already examined some of "the oleanders of life"—the flowering, that is, of this extemporary genius who supplied generations of Williams students with firewood, apples, and gilt-edge fender-dented delirious oratory. Bill Pratt played the mouth organ, and his brilliant spoken syllables (*munification*, *polidity*, *opodildoc*, *bluce*) lapped across each other the way one slides along in saliva over the face of the instrument. But even common words uncommonly ordered could survive:

"Good evening, Mr. ——, I hope you have a superfluous and peculiar predestination." "No, Bill, no time to talk this evening." "But your resolution is not affected, I hope, Sir." "Not in the least, Bill." "Well, Sir, perhaps you are preoccupied with removal?" "That's just it, Bill, so you had better move along." "But, Sir, perhaps if you do not care for music and the circumferences of my hymoniky, you would like the lonely digestion of a peck of apples?"

Bill Pratt, the frugal enthusiast, was apparently no traveller. He fervently hoped to visit Pittsfield (which to him was *Pitchfield*) but he never did. However, he always spoke with the total universe in mind; and his random remarks, if you have generously considered them on the previous page, seem to fit Katahdin Falls as if he were speaking right on the spot. "If I had to read the sign-boards," he once remarked, "I never could get out of Williamstown."

KATAHDIN FALLS, MAINE

The boy and girl in the upper right will give you an idea of the size of these falls. They run into the West Branch of the Penobscot River at the base of Mt. Katahdin. You follow the stream from the Katahdin Stream campground on the southwest side of Baxter State Park. The Appalachian Trail follows the Hunt Spur to the Tableland (3-1/2 miles) and on to the Baxter Peak (5.2 miles). Only a mile up this trail are the beautiful falls. From many points along this trail are outstanding views of the lakes and streams below. Needless to say I brought the models along with me, for you just couldn't hope to find hikers without waiting for hours.

Exposure—1/10 of a second at f:14. ASA Speed 50.

ARTHUR GRIFFIN

A World So Gilded

There were two things I noticed and marveled at in my new world. One of these was the sun and the other was the air. I had never seen a world so gilded and so richly bathed and blessed by such a benign sun as that world was by that sun. The sun seemed to pour down a lavish, golden, invulnerable contentment on everything, on people, houses, animals, fields—and a sweetness like the sweetness of passion. The sun had so much room to shine in there. It had the whole sky to shine in, and it had miles and miles of hills and woods, it had islands and rocks and boats to glisten on and soak into like oil. And it was thanks to the matchless air of that peninsula that such a flood of sunshine never became a burden. It always seemed exactly right, golden and voluptuous yet without weight. It was as if the air there were so buoyant that it always lifted up part of the weight of the sun's heat and kept it from ever falling too heavily on our shoulders. It was indescribable air. It made every day seem like a gala day. We never woke up to an ordinary humdrum morning.

I noticed these two things, the air and the sun, at my own house more than I had ever noticed them at the other end of the town. I imagined that the reason for this was that my house responded to sun and air more than most houses do. Sometimes it felt like a boat at anchor. There is that curious quality about all the little noises on a boat which makes them sound unmistakably boaty. The tapping of a rope against canvas, the squeak of a pulley, a voice or a footstep heard on a boat are different from the same sounds heard on land. They are magnified and yet softened by the sea air. All such little noises around my house struck me as having that same soft boaty sound. A clothespin dropped on the doorstep had it, and the rustle of a curtain in an open window sounded like a sail fluttering. When the window sill burned my fingers on a hot morning it was just as if I had touched the gunwale of a dory that had been lying in the sun for hours.

KATHARINE BUTLER HATHAWAY

"What beautiful things we leave behind," said Charles William Eliot, twenty-first President of Harvard. To Sarah Orne Jewett, the old world of New England—at any rate, the old world along the seacoast of Maine—was falling apart by 1881. With sentiment controlled, yet full at times of heartbreak in what to our tough century must seem an unheartbroken day between the wars, Miss Jewett speaks with level voice. And with affection. She was as much at home in a small boat as she was in her country-doctor father's carriage or in the saddle, galloping "when wind whistles in my ears." And for all her reserve, poise, dignity, and love of solitude, she was at home with people, especially older people. And in such a town as this.

A single poplar may have a severe and uncharitable look, but a row of them suggests the antique and pleasing pomp and ceremony of their early days, before the sideboard cupboards were only used to keep the boxes of strings and nails and the duster; and the best decanters were put on a high shelf, while the plain ones were used for vinegar in the kitchen closet. There is far less social visiting from house to house than there used to be. People in the smaller towns have more acquaintances who live at a distance than was the case before the days of railroads, and there are more guests who come from a distance, which has something to do with making tea-parties and the entertainment of one's neighbors less frequent than in former times. But most of the New England towns have changed their characters in the last twenty years, since the manufactories have come in and brought together large numbers either of foreigners or of a different class of people from those who used to make the most of the population. A certain class of families is rapidly becoming extinct. There will be found in the older villages very few persons left who belong to this class, which was once far more important and powerful; the oldest churches are apt to be most thinly attended simply because a different sort of ideas, even of heavenly things, attract the newer residents. I suppose that elderly people have said, ever since the time of Shem, Ham, and Japhet's wives in the ark, that society is nothing to what it used to be, and we may expect to be always told what unworthy successors we are of our grandmothers. But the fact remains that a certain element of American society is fast dying out, giving place to the new; and with all our glory and pride in modern progress and success we cling to the old associations regretfully. There is nothing to take the place of the pleasure we have in going to see our old friends in the parlors which have changed little since our childhood.

(Sarah Orne Jewett)

NEW HARBOR, MAINE

Before the Pilgrim Fathers set foot upon the sands of Cape Cod, English fishermen and traders had stations on Pemaquid Point. When Captain John Smith was at Monhegan in 1614, he noted vessels coming out of the harbor. Here at New Harbor lived the famous chieftain Samoset who, from the English traders, learned enough of the strange tongue to surprise the Plymouth settlers with his "Much welcome, Englishmen." Around the mouth of the harbor at the right is Back Cove, an ideal subject for pictures and paintings. A few miles on is Pemaquid Point where ground swells roll in against the rocks after a storm and the gulls will almost eat out of your hand if you are enjoying a picnic or fishing off the rocky cliffs. There's also a replica of part of ancient Fort William Henry on a knoll above Pemaquid Beach, overlooking Johns Island. I went out five mornings in a row, rising at 4 A.M. to capture this sunrise. The first four mornings the sun overslept. In the summer in New England, the sun rises a bit after four o'clock. I hate getting up in the morning, but each time I have, I have enjoyed the silence and the leisurely coming of light. Everything is quiet (with the exception of busy harbors). Suddenly where there was just brightness the sun appears. Sunrises are more difficult to judge, for they are the reverse of sunsets. Often the best color is before the sun actually appears. If you wait until you see the sun, you may go back to bed very unhappy.

Exposure—1/10 of a second at f:14. ASA Speed 50.

ARTHUR GRIFFIN

Not Merely Ancestors

But here I cannot but stay and make a pause, and stand half amazed at this poor people's present condition; and so I think will the reader, too, when he well considers the same. Being thus passed the vast ocean, and a sea of troubles before in their preparation (as may be remembered by that which went before), they had now no friends to welcome them nor inns to entertain or refresh their weatherbeaten bodies; no houses or much less towns to repair to, to seek for succour. It is recorded in Scripture as a mercy to the Apostle and his shipwrecked company, that the barbarians showed them no small kindness in refreshing them, but these savage barbarians, when they met with them (as after will appear) were readier to fill their sides full of arrows than otherwise. And for the season it was winter, and they that know the winters of that country know them to be sharp and violent, and subject to cruel and fierce storms, dangerous to travel to known places, much more to search an unknown coast. Besides, what could they see but a hideous and desolate wilderness, fall of wild beasts and wild men—and what multitudes there might be of them they knew not. Neither could they, as it were, go up to the top of Pisgah to view from this wilderness a more goodly country to feed their hopes; for which way soever they turned their eyes (save upward to the heavens) they could have little solace or content in respect of any outward objects. For summer being done, all things stand upon them with a weatherbeaten face, and the whole country, full of woods and thickets, represented a wild and savage hue. If they looked behind them, there was the mighty ocean which they had passed and was now as a main bar and gulf to separate them from all the civil parts of the world. If it be said they had a ship to succour them, it is true; but what heard they daily from the master and company? But that with speed they should look out a place (with their shallop) where they would be, at some near distance; for the season was such as he would not stir from thence till a safe harbor was discovered by them, where they would be, and he might go without danger; and that victuals consumed apace but he must and would keep sufficient for themselves and their return.

WILLIAM BRADFORD

As a non-fiction writer—by which I mean one who does not even attempt to write fiction—I should point out that the Bradford passage implies a view of *Mayflower II* on almost wintry seas. Arthur Griffin's engaging study was made in summer. And as a trustee of the Plimouth Plantation, I should be derelict in my loyalty if I failed to mention the fascination of this full-scale replica when one sees and boards her for the first time. As we go to press, something like a million and a half men, women, and children, visiting Plymouth, Massachusetts, have walked her decks, and below deck, and marveled that in the end so small and frail a vessel should ever have raised that memorable landfall on the hem of this continent.

Stephen Vincent Benét's posthumous *Western Star* was published in 1943, the year of his death. This was Book One of a multi-book project beginning with the famous voyage that began in September:

> So think of them through the sixty-five long days
> Of tempest and fair weather, of calm and storm,
> They were not yet Pilgrim Fathers in steeple-hats,
> Each with an iron jaw and a musketoon,
> They were not Pilgrim Mothers, sure of their fame.
> They were men and women and children, cramped in a ship,
> Bound for an unknown land and wondering.
>
> The godly prayed, the ungodly spat overside,
> The sailors jeered now and then at the pious speeches,
> The Billington boys behaved like limbs of Satan,
> And the three pregnant women walked the decks
> Or lay in their cabins, wondering at night
> What hour their pains would strike and what would be born.
> In fact, there were human beings aboard the *Mayflower*,
> Not merely ancestors.
>
> *(Stephen Vincent Benét)*

MAYFLOWER II APPROACHING THE NEW WORLD

When I made this picture of Mayflower II *100 miles out to sea, I had no idea the following thirty hours would be the most frightening in my photographic career. We had taken more than two days to find the Mayflower, on her way from Plymouth, England, to Plymouth, America, cruising with Richard Robie on his yacht* Sea Doll. *Just after taking my pictures one of our engines died, and then the other, right in the middle of the shipping lane. A U.S. destroyer fired a line over our bow and towed us to the Nantucket Lightship just in time, as shortly afterwards the S.S.* United States *sailed by, and our* Sea Doll *practically stood on end. At eleven o'clock that night the Coast Guard started to tow us to Woods Hole in a very, very heavy sea. During the fourteen hours the thick tow line broke three times. Each time one of us had to crawl to the bow to catch and fasten another line. Later the Coast Guard told us that they thought that the* Sea Doll *might break in half. We all knew when we reached Woods Hole how the pilgrims felt when they sighted land, but we didn't have Indians waiting as a reception committee. Handheld, roll-film camera.*

Exposure, 1/100 of a second at f:16. ASA Speed 50.

ARTHUR GRIFFIN

Lay of the Land

When you rise a hill to overlook a bold prospect, can anybody persuade you that your horse does not enjoy the sight too? His ears go forward, his eye lights up with a large and bright look, and he gazes for a moment with equine enthusiasm, till some succulent bough or grassy tuft converts his taste into a physical form. A good horse is a perfect gentleman. He meets you in the morning with unmistakable pleasure; if you are near the grain-bin, he will give you the most cordial invitation, if not to breakfast with him, at least to wait upon him in that interesting ceremony. His drinking is particularly nice. He always loves running water, in the clearest brook, at the most sparkling place in it. No man shall make me believe that he does not observe and quietly enjoy the sun-flash on the gravel beneath, and on the wavy surface above. He arches down his neck to the surface, his mane falls gracefully over his head, he drinks with hearty earnestness, and the throbbing swallows pulsate so audibly and musically that you feel a sympathetic thirst. Now he lifts his head, and looks first up the road to see who is coming, and then down the road, at those work-horses, turned loose, affecting gayety with their old stiff legs and hooped bellies, and then, with a long breath, he takes the after-drink. Once more lifting his head, but now only a few inches above the surface, the drops trickle from his lips back to the brook. Finally, he cleanses his mouth, and chews his bit, and plays with the surface of the water with his lithe lip, and begins to paw the stream.

HENRY WARD BEECHER

One small object which I cherish stands on a certain bookcase where I can easily see it. It is a large Staffordshire cup, signed *Adams England*. It measures four and three-quarters inches across and three and one-half inches deep. On one side the farmer's arms stand out in color: "In God is Our Trust"; a shock of golden wheat; a sickle, not a scythe. Let into the sides of the central arms circle are four smaller circles displaying the tools of husbandry all nicely entwined with twelve lines of verse. There are flowers and leaves on the handle, and leaves and flowers braided inside the lip of the cup. On the reverse of the outside the poem appears a second time, lettered after an ancient face of type and ornamented with what must be a wine cask or cider barrel and a bottle and glass. Walter de la Mare somewhere speaks of "Mr Anonymous." Mr Anonymous is the author of some of the best rhyming witchery in the English language; but he never did better than here. I quote his inspiration because it levels (in the modern sense) with the farmer; and the farmer has not always leveled with those who ride to hounds.

> Let the Wealthy & Great,
> Roll in Splendor & State,
> I envy them not I declare it:
> I eat my own Lamb,
> My Chickens and Ham,
> I shear my own Fleece & I wear it.
> I have Lawns, I have Bow'rs,
> I have Fruits, I have Flow'rs,
> The Lark is my morning alarmer:
> So jolly Boys now,
> Here's God speed the Plough,
> Long Life & success to the Farmer.
>
> *(Anonymous)*

MYOPIA HUNT CLUB, NORTH SHORE, MASSACHUSETTS

This picture which reminds me of an old English print, was taken at one of the annual race meetings of the Myopia Hunt Club. Such was the only occasion when the Duke of Windsor, when he was Prince of Wales, rode with the hunt in America. Long-time Master of the Fox Hounds, Frederic Winthrop, and his whipper-in were getting the hounds in line when this beautiful lighting appeared. Mr. Winthrop is the tenth generation of his family to farm the land originally granted to Governor Winthrop of the Massachusetts Bay Colony. I made this with my roll-film camera hand-held.

Exposure—1/100 of a second at f:11. ASA Speed 50.

Of Barnacles and Boats

At low tide the barnacle-covered rocks seem a mineral landscape carved and sculptured into millions of little sharply pointed cones. There is no movement, no sign or suggestion of life. The stony shells, like those of mollusks, are calcareous and are secreted by the invisible animals within. Each cone-shaped shell consists of six neatly fitted plates forming an encircling ring. A covering door of four plates closes to protect the barnacle from drying when the tide has ebbed, or swings open to allow it to feed. The first ripples of incoming tide bring the petrified fields to life. Then if one stands ankle-deep in water and observes closely, one sees tiny shadows flickering everywhere over the submerged rocks. Over each individual cone, a feathered plume is regularly thrust out and drawn back within the slightly opened portals of the central door—the rhythmic motions by which the barnacle sweeps in diatoms and other microscopic life of the returning sea.

The creature inside each shell is something like a small pinkish shrimp that lies head downward, firmly cemented to the base of this chamber it cannot leave. Only the appendages are ever exposed—six pairs of branched, slender wands, jointed and set with bristles. Acting together, they form a net of great efficiency.

RACHEL CARSON

I have never cared greatly for photographs of harbors with boats tied to wharves or stacked not unlike the sardines they sometimes profess to seine for. It follows that Rachel Carson should be talking about barnacles, which these pilings and stones of course suggest. It may be that readers of her brief observation will look for themselves (as shall I) to see the life, or the shadow of life, to which she so vividly directs our half-closed eyes.

This would be the moment to say that my concern as dredger of these serial extracts from their country sleep may seem to have shifted my interest from the photographs themselves. Such is not the case. Arthur Griffin's voyage in color has made my own passage deeply rewarding—and rewarding I hope to others. It is his deck chair I am sitting in at sea, his mountain that I climb ashore, his valley opening for me while I perch upon an old rail fence. The making of pictures is one thing, the cutting for composition still another, and the work of preparation for the press quite something else. It was the publisher who elected that we choose the principal quotations from authors no longer alive; but my notes on those authors have trespassed into the property of the living. I wish the dead could see what a fine lens artist with modern techniques under instant control can do in apposition to their words which were always under control, else they would be of little use to us here, and of very small interest to anyone. Five of those writers, incidentally, were photographed by Arthur Griffin in the days when he was working on national magazine assignments. The five were Sinclair Lewis, Lucien Price, Bernard DeVoto, Wilbur Cross, and Ferris Greenslet. He has also made several fine studies of Henry Beston.

STONINGTON, CONNECTICUT

Little remains of the early shipbuilding which made Stonington a bustling center in the Colony of Connecticut. Then the village was popularly known as a "Nursery for Seamen." One of the first whaling franchises granted in America was issued for the waters between Stonington and Montauk Point. Today Stonington is a quiet town of modest, shady streets. Off the Boston Post Road on a long point it juts into the ocean and is rich in magnificent marine views. There remains an atmosphere of whaling days. Large white Colonial houses of former sea captains, a white church, and row after row of elms that cast long shadows add to its attractiveness. Walking to the end of the point you pass through Cannon Square, where stand two of the guns used in the defense of Stonington against the British attack of 1812, and the stone lighthouse, two excellent camera subjects.

Exposure—1/10 of a second at f:30. ASA Speed 50.

ARTHUR GRIFFIN

FALL

Stone Walls

We circled a hill on which a white church-tower rose so high
above the trees that it made the sky seem nearer the earth
than it was. Then we were among the clean meadows and
white houses and barns again, and always in sight of stone
walls—stone walls that separated meadow from woodland,
pasture from orchard, roadway and lane from paddock.
Houses built on granite foundations, where they belonged,
and boulder walls everywhere gave a tonic look of perma-
nency to the landscape. That one's race ever should have
had the toughness of fiber to establish themselves in these
hills in any fashion is a heavy entry to their credit. But that
they should have had the endurance to do it so permanently
is little short of miraculous. Once I computed what the
stone walls on three New Hampshire farms would cost at
prevailing prices for wall building—to say nothing of the
cost of digging and prying the boulders out of the fields and
getting them to where they were needed—and the walls
would have cost from two to three times what the farms
with all late improvements added were worth at the highest
market prices.

ROLLO WALTER BROWN

To the midwesterner, the plainsman, the man from west of the continental divide, nothing on the New England landscape can be so impressive as the endless miles and miles of old stone walls. Even in the back country of the north, where second growth and second mortgages long since took over, the walls run their lonely broken course, hospitable to moss and lichen and to those few summer vagrants out in search of cellar holes, the lost but stubborn apple tree or lilac, and raspberries run wild. Rollo Walter Brown came to New England from Ohio. He was tall, gaunt, big-limbed, making the statues of Abraham Lincoln seem more plausible. Did any of us catch him in the hefting of a boulder? If ever a kindly man was built for mending walls, it was most surely he. I suppose he is remembered best for *The Creative Spirit*; but I still think *How the French Boy Learns to Write* his most original book. Perhaps even better is that pair of brief biographies of his father and mother, one of which appeared in *Harper's*, the other in the *Atlantic*.

He has made a shrewd observation. Useless, perhaps, but shrewd. What millions of man-hours must have accounted for the clearing of resistant fields, the building of New England walls!

> The sevenfield length of boulders, moon-limbed and starry,
> Spilled from the dead of night and the vault-blue quarry,
> Lies in the fallows, brambled and catenary.
>
> Some of them sprung from the age-old graveyard socketing,
> Where the first rueful settler found them pocketing
> As when original void had sent them rocketing.
>
> These are the crib-stones now, or the boundary finders
> Out of the century cleaned of its hard reminders
> Since the last ox is gone, and the horse with blinders . . .

GRAFTON, VERMONT

*I have found in the southern section of Vermont an unlimited source of color pictures. Newfane, Townshend, Wardsboro and Grafton, to mention a few, convey New England in most peaceful settings. This area is really unspoiled and also unknown to the average tourist. Grafton, Newfane and Woodstock are especially charming villages. Driving past this lane one bright fall morning I was aware that the color was fairly good, but not quite brilliant enough to stop and photograph.
I returned that afternoon and you can see what I saw. What makes this picture is the side-back lighting. Without this the color would be flat, with no depth at all and not worth shooting.*

Exposure—1/25 of a second at f:16. ASA Speed 50.

110

Marshfield and Daniel Webster

(Mrs. Grace Webster to James W. Paige)
Sandwich [Mass.] Sept. 6, 1826.

MY DEAR BROTHER,
***Mr. W. has just returned from the field [to day] with more than one feather to day. He went out with Mr. Child and usual attendants to the great marshes and brought home 70 large birds—Mr. W. shot 46 with his own hand, consisting as I hear the catalogue of ring-tailed curlews, Beetle-heads, red breasts, Humilitys and greybeaks—much the greatest part being red breasts. He is very tired or he would write to Mr. Blake. he says he burnt all his powder—fired away all his shot, broke his ram-rod—got no dinner, and walked a long way on the Marshes after they were covered with the tide—he wishes you to tell Mr. B. that he never saw better shooting in the great marshes—and that if he had known where the birds were to be found—he might have gone directly to them with a chaise.

     ᴢ   ᴢ   ᴢ   ᴢ

(George Ticknor to Prescott)

Summer. 1828
***But Mr. Webster is a true sportsman. He was out 13 hours today, without any regular meal, and is now as busy as a locksmith, with his guns. He seems to feel as if it were the one thing needful to kill birds and neither to tire or grow hungry while one can be seen. It has already made him look bright and strong again, for he came from Nantucket in but a poor condition. . . .

     ᴢ   ᴢ   ᴢ   ᴢ

(To Porter Wright)

April 16, [1848?]

PORTER WRIGHT
I thought it was *Asa* Delano, the Carpenter, not *Nathl*, who wanted to go into the John Taylor House. Mr. Nat Delano is an excellent man, & I like him much—& is very handy with a Boat; but he has always a gun in his hand, & if he lives in that house, he will kill every quail, for 6 miles all around,—& not leave one for me. I do not wish to say this to him, exactly; but I do not incline to let him in. You may say, that I prefer letting it to those who work altogether on the Farm.

Yrs D. W.

From or About DANIEL WEBSTER

On 29 September 1840 Daniel Webster added a postscript to a letter to his wife: "I got up once or twice to look out—today is lovely Oh, Marshfield! —Marshfield!"

The greatest all-round fisherman I ever knew—and Ferris Greenslet pays tribute to him in *Under the Bridge*—was the painter, Leslie P. Thompson, N.A. His book called *Fishing in New England*, printed in England in 1955 by the Chiswick Press, contains the author's lifetime observations on trout stream insects, the artificial fly, accurately and exquisitely illustrated in delicate watercolor. But his range of fishing experience extended from trout to smelt, to striped bass and carp. He himself on a kernel of stewed corn took one carp from the dubious waters of the Charles River which weighed in excess of eighteen pounds—eighteen pounds, one ounce, to be exact: "20 June 1939: Medfield meadows: Water low and reasonably clear: Cloudy, warm, clearing after rain in the morning."

It was not "Oh, Marshfield!" which Let Thompson exclaimed. He would never exclaim; but he would *think* "North River!" which for him was practically the same thing. A typical Thompson soliloquy along another stretch of the tidal stream at which you are looking:

My beat begins at the old wharf two hundred yards down river where I start to cast. It is pleasant to hear the distant plop and sometimes see the splash of the lead at the end of the cast. The first fish is a three-pounder, and his coming and going is felt rather than seen; an eery business is the playing of a fish at night. In a short time he is led over the flooded grass, the hook is gently removed and he swims away. During the morning we have seen signs of larger fish in this stretch of the river, and I am not disappointed when the next two fish are brought ashore, for the flashlight shows a trifle over seven pounds when each is held on the spring balance. With water over the grass, the gaff is not brought into play, but its four-foot shaft helps considerably when walking the flooded banks. Both fish are knocked on the head and strung on the stout thong of elk-hide. The almanac has warned us of an uncommonly high tide, and I am not surprised when I find the water close to the top of my knee boots. Working up the bank I come to the mouth of a familiar ditch—now invisible—but the long gaff handle feels the edge. One more cast before I retreat, and I'm fast to a third fish, and when strung on the lanyard with his mates, they are alike as peas in a pod. It's high time to gain dry ground, and trailing a burden of over twenty pounds, I throw care to the winds and with boots full of water join my companion up river.

(Leslie P. Thompson)

MARSHFIELD, MASSACHUSETTS

This picture was made in the latter part of the duck season. In years gone by this marsh was one of the best known shooting areas on the South Shore. The federal government is now considering making an area close by a preserve. Black duck are shot in the early season and red legs and whistlers in the late season. I took this picture a couple of hours after sunrise. To get to this spot, we made a long perilous hike in pitch darkness over wet, cold marshland. You could fall into a deep hole or ditch at any step, but we had to set out the decoys and hide before dawn. The sunrise wasn't too colorful, so I saved the morning by taking pictures of the setting out of decoys and other studies.

Exposure—1/25 of a second at f:22. ASA Speed 50.

ARTHUR GRIFFIN

Concord Hymn

By the rude bridge that arched the flood,
　　Their flag to April's breeze unfurled,
Here once the embattled farmers stood,
　　And fired the shot heard round the world.

The foe long since in silence slept;
　　Alike the conqueror silent sleeps;
And Time the ruined bridge has swept
　　Down the dark stream that seaward creeps.

On this green bank, by this soft stream,
　　We set to-day a votive stone;
That memory may their deed redeem,
　　When, like our sires, our sons are gone.

Spirit, that made those heroes dare
　　To die, and leave their children free,
Bid Time and Nature gently spare
　　The shaft we raise to them and thee.

RALPH WALDO EMERSON

Emerson's "Concord Hymn" was sung to the tune of "Old Hundred" at the completion of the Battle Monument on July 4, 1837—the year in which Thoreau was graduated from Harvard. The local newspaper of the day said it was written by a Concord citizen. Anonymity sustained the bullet in its solo orbit; but it is Emerson who gave the moment immortality.

The rude bridge itself—the North Bridge by name—was torn down in 1794 but re-erected in 1875 for the dedication of the Minute-Man statue. Replacements (one of concrete) have been washed out at least three times. The hurricane of 1938 did for the concrete. The present structure is again of wood.

The statue, by Daniel Chester French, was his first important work. Among other memorable statues executed by this sculptor is that of John Harvard which stands in front of University Hall in the College Yard in *Cambridge*. Emerson was graduated from *Harvard* in 1821; Paul Revere's ride really started from the gleam of those two lanterns "aloft in the belfry arch of the North Church tower" in *Boston*. In the summer of 1913, writing of Cambridge from Boston to the *Westminster Gazette*, Rupert Brooke concluded—though likely not with the above facts in mind—"Harvard, Boston, New England, it is impossible to say how much they are interwoven, and how they have influenced America."

NORTH BRIDGE, CONCORD, MASSACHUSETTS

I had photographed Concord's Old North Bridge many times over the years in the other three seasons, but never bothered to go there for fall color. You can imagine my surprise to find this brilliant setting almost in my own back yard, while driving home from a couple of weeks of fall foliage shooting in Vermont and New Hampshire. A year before Robert Frost passed away, he told me that Emerson's poem of the "Rude Bridge" was his favorite, and that he had made many visits to Concord to meditate in this peaceful setting. We had planned on going out some afternoon to get a color picture of him on the bridge, but just didn't make it. In the background of this shot you can see the bronze figure of a Minute Man leaving his plow for the wars. This was the first masterpiece of 21-year-old Concord sculptor, Daniel Chester French, whose Lincoln Memorial is world famous.

Exposure—1/10 of a second at f:22. ASA Speed 50.

ARTHUR GRIFFIN

Far and Near

Late in the evening I started on to Foligno in order to take a train in to Rome for Easter morning. I followed a white road that wound around the hills, through silent clusters of cottages tightly shut up with only a slit of light visible now and then, meeting not a human being along the way save three somber figures accompanying an ox cart, a man at the head of the oxen and a man and woman at the tail of the cart—a theme for Millet. (I asked in broken Italian how far it was to Foligno, and the answer was, "*Una hora*"—distance in time and not in miles.) Off in the night I could see the lights of Perugia, and some time after midnight I began to see the lights of Foligno—of Perugia and Foligno, where Raphael had wandered and painted. The adventure of it all was that when I reached Foligno I found that it was a walled town, that the gate was shut, and that I had neither passport nor intelligible speech. There is an interesting walking sequel to this journey. I carried that night a wooden water-bottle, such as the Italian soldiers used to carry, filling it from the fountain at the gate of Assisi before starting. Just a month later, under the same full moon, I was walking between midnight and morning in New Hampshire. I had the same water-bottle and stopped at a spring to fill it. When I turned the bottle upside down, a few drops of water from the fountain of Assisi fell into the New England spring, which for me, at any rate, has been forever sweetened by this association.

JOHN FINLEY

Once or twice I had the pleasure of walking up town in my native New York with Mr. Finley, whose older son (my vintage) was later to hook and land a five-pound squaretail in my presence on Kennebago Stream. Where Mr. Finley was walking that morning, I can't recall. His destination was the New York *Times* of which he was then either Associate Editor or Editor-in-Chief. Actually, he was stepping off some miles in England, France, or even farther afield: a precise distance which he would transfer at home to the map of his vicarious journey: a cumulative walk of days and weeks or months. It was in some such way that, crossing the channel by proxy, Hilaire Belloc walked to Rome. Here, in the distance, you can see New Hampshire. But you can't see Tamworth, where Mr. Finley summered.

PEACHAM, VERMONT

Roads to Peacham run uphill, for this pastoral land is in high country near where the Connecticut and the Passumpsic rivers join. Peacham is at an elevation of approximately 1900 feet. It is a tree-shaded town of old white houses, many of them now owned by folk from all over the country who come and spend the summer—especially college professors. Peacham Academy, which boasts scores of distinguished graduates, is at the right of my scene. Thad Stevens, who made Peacham internationally famous, lived and studied here. This is one of my favorite Vermont hill villages. From the high field behind the large Congregational church there are breathtaking views of the valley with the hills and mountains beyond. This picture, made on an unusually clear afternoon, shows the Presidential Range, capped with snow, some forty miles away.

Exposure—1/25 of a second at f:22. ASA Speed 50.

ARTHUR GRIFFIN

Northeast Kingdom

What we love, when on a summer day we step into the cool-ness of a wood, is that its boughs close up behind us. We are escaped, into another room of life. The wood does not live as we live, restless and running, panting after flesh, and even in sleep tossing with fears. It is aloof from thoughts and instincts; it responds, but only to the sun and wind, the rock and the stream—never, though you shout yourself hoarse, to propaganda, temptation, reproach, or promises. You cannot mount a rock and preach to a tree how it shall attain the kingdom of heaven. It is already closer to it, up there, than you will grow to be. And you cannot make it see the light, since in the tree's sense you are blind. You have nothing to bring it, for all the forest is self-sufficient; if you burn it, cut, hack through it with a blade, it angrily repairs the swathe with thorns and weeds and fierce suckers. Later there are good green leaves again, toiling, adjusting, breath-ing—forgetting you.

For this green living is the world's primal industry; yet it makes no roar. Waving its banners, it marches across the earth and the ages, without dust around its columns. I do not hold that all of that life is pretty; it is not, in purpose, sprung for us, and moves under no compulsion to please. If ever you fought with thistles, or tried to pull up a cattail's matted rootstocks, you will know how plants cling to their own lives and defy you. The pond-scums gather in the cis-tern, frothing and buoyed with their own gases; the storm waves fling at your feet upon the beach the limp sea-lettuce wrenched from its submarine hold—reminder that there too, where the light is filtered and refracted, there is life still to intercept and net and by it proliferate.

DONALD CULROSS PEATTIE

Access to Willoughby Lake should be forbidden except through that gate in the south—the huge and unexpected passage between Pisgah and Hor. I first passed through it in the company of Arthur Pease. We had moved in on it gradually from Randolph, New Hampshire—see page 131—across the Connecticut River, stopping frequently to examine stations of balm of gilead, sweet grass, bedstraw, penny cress, swamp botany, and other flourishing excitements. I was unprepared for Lake Willoughby in spite of what my guide had told me about it. Let me speak only of the clearest water ever waded into, and the law forbidding one to shoot the operator of a huge fiber-glass outboard job in mad acrobatics, disturbing as a plane-crash in the dining room.

Littleton, in my fervent fishing days, was to me a familiar town; it reminds me now of what Thomas Hill wrote in 1848 about a collecting trip with Louis Agassiz when the railroad was first opened up the Ammonoosuc valley. In the party were Cornelius C. Felton, his two brothers, Samuel (Superintendent of the Fitchburg Railroad, known to Kipling) and John B.; two professors; Agassiz, and his young son just arrived from Europe with not a word of English. Agile with a butterfly net, the boy would rally to the cry, "*Beau Papillon!*"

From Littleton we took stages for Franconia Notch. There was but one other passenger in the coach, an exceedingly solemn-looking man, and very silent. He was apparently shocked by the levity and gayety of our party; who, although on science bent, all had a cheerful mind. When we came to the foot of a long hill, we all got out and walked, except Professor Cornelius Felton who remained on the seat with the driver. As we were turning over stones and sticks, for hidden reptiles or insects; looking on the under side of leaves to discover butterflies, or snails; rapping the bushes, to start little moths, and occasionally shouting one to another "Beau Papillon"; the driver asked Professor Felton who these men were, that were with him. He replied "they are a set of naturalists, from an institution near Boston."

Our zoological pursuits retarded our movements up the hill so much that the coach had got far ahead of us, and our van was led by the solemn man, who had not taken any part in our performances. As we drew near the top of the hill, however, a remarkably beautiful butterfly went in front of him. The flush of his boyhood seemed instantly to return. He took off his hat, and made a sweep for it; and as the butterfly easily eluded him, he made a second and a third; growing more and more eager, till, at length, as the butterfly rose and soared over a high clump of bushes, our solemn man leaped into the air, made his last frantic swoop, and screamed, at the top of his voice, "Beau Papillon." At that moment, the stage in the opposite direction met ours, at the top of the hill. The drivers paused a moment to exchange salutations, and the other said to ours, "Why! You've a strange freight down there. Who are they?" Our driver, leaning toward him, said in a confidential whisper. "They are a set of naturals from that insane asylum near Boston. Their keeper just told me so."

(*Thomas Hill*)

126

LAKE WILLOUGHBY, VERMONT

Lake Willoughby is far up in the Northeast Kingdom of Vermont. This region is a favored haunt for artists and photographers, but so far off the beaten track that not many tourists visit it. The vision of Willoughby comes with a sudden grandeur that is rare in the usually serene Vermont landscape. Here the mighty plow of glacial ice sheared through a barrier of granite mountain, and gouging deep into the earth, left a cold and lovely lake lying in between the stark cliffs of Pisgah and Hor (left to right in my view). The inevitable comparison of Willoughby to the lakes of Switzerland gave rise to the title, "The Lucerne of America." This title is not needed, however, to stamp Willoughby apart from the other lakes of Vermont and New England. Without back-lighting my picture would have been quite flat and uninteresting. I first saw this composition at high noon and returned to get it in more favorable light. I got a bonus in the dark dramatic sky.

Exposure—1/25 of a second at f:14. ASA Speed 50.

ARTHUR GRIFFIN

Sundews and Leatherleaf

One might also be tempted to reflect a little upon the almost unvarying nature and equipment of the boats upon such a pond as this. Given a small lake in northern New England you may safely predict of it the following details: a narrow but well-trodden footpath, squirming through a thicket of untrimmed alders and other bushes and becoming peatier and wetter underfoot as it nears the edge of the pond. Second, moored by a rusty chain to the decayed trunk of an old pine tree waterlogged at the edge of the lake, and with sundews and leatherleaf growing in its deep lengthwise cracks, is to be found a flat-bottomed boat, once painted green, partly filled with accumulated rain water. In its bow is a piece of old clothesline tied around a heavy stone for an anchor; amidships rests a worn and broken oar remade into a paddle; on one seat or floating in the wet bottom a tin can for bailing, and, in the most watery parts, a few bloated angleworms, which have somehow been frustrated in their subterranean mission but have not attained the compensation of a vermicular Nirvana in the throat or stomach of a fish. Over all this craft and its equipment hovers the aroma of fishes and other fishes and still more fishes which have been through the seasons landed and cleaned in it. A few grace notes may be added, such as an extra can or two, an empty bottle, and a fishhook carefully stuck into the side of the boat, and then you may multiply this picture n times along our northern lakes and bogs.

ARTHUR STANLEY PEASE

Arthur Stanley Pease, Harvard graduate, classicist and sometime President of Amherst College, was a self-taught botanist of such learning and enthusiasm that to walk with him afield in New Hampshire or Vermont or Maine was a kind of atonement for all that one had missed through willful blindness. His humbly written essays appearing in *Appalachia*, or gathered in *Sequestered Vales of Life*, or just that Waumbek fragment (Waumbek: Indian for *mountain*) on the preceding page, are the man himself. Four plants are named for him. In a lifetime of summers in Randolph, north of tall Mount Madison, he might one rainy day be reminded to tell you, as he glanced toward the fading Pilot Range, that he had climbed in all some 200 different mountains in the region—not a few of them many times. He looked like Calvin Coolidge, the small round mouth and all; but he walked, talked, and even dressed like some plain homespun Dante out of Littleton. Simple, good, great, generous, shy, alert—with the driest of wit, the faintest twinkle of a smile—may some who knew him read this in remembrance. And may others believe there was and could be such a man. And may this follower who loved him as a friend still see him almost vaulting at three-score-sixteen years across that fence in Freyburg, five miles or so from the picture opposite, to explain that the pink spring-growth in a pool of casual water, which made it look like a dish of fresh stewed rhubarb, was (with no apology for Latin or one's ignorance) *glycerea borealis*. There is even a way to impart knowledge that is poetry itself.

KEZAR LAKE, CENTER LOVELL, MAINE

This is a lovely lake just a few miles from the New Hampshire border. Its pine-clad shores shelter splendid summer homes and one lodge which the AAA rates as outstanding—one of the few with that top rating in New England. The panorama in the background is part of the White Mountain National Forest. Driving into Maine from here is like a speedy trip through Europe. You pass through Sweden, Denmark, Poland, Norway, Naples and Paris. If you become bored with these, keep on going to Mexico, Canton, China, Lisbon, Vienna and Rome.

Exposure—1/25 of a second at f:22. ASA Speed 50.

ARTHUR GRIFFIN

Under the Bridge

But the brook is not for the eye alone; it is the string of a mighty violin, stretched between the mountains and the sea. And it has a great gamut, from the broad rumbling bass of the main current rounding a granite boulder to the tiny trebles of little ripples sparkling pizzicato in the shallows. Where the stream flows wide over gravel beds there are numberless singers blending their tones like so many leaves in a tree, but where it narrows and bores between rocky walls the voices crowd together in one vague shout. Comes a fall, and the shout deepens to a roar, overlaid by faint screams and splashings and by tones that sound in desolate places like those of the human voice calling from far away. Below the fall there is heard, underneath the sound of steady onrush, a half-drowned subaqueous grumbling from the under-tow as of some giant tossing there, and a clamor of somersaulting currents that boil upward and break out-ward into the day. Every bubble of the thousands bursting here adds its particle to the tumult, and the long sigh of the current slipping past reeds at the stream's edge is added also. One hundred feet farther down the water quiets into a pool. All the uproar becomes an echo, then a memory. There is only the faint ruffling of the breeze on the backs of the ripples. But at the sill of the pool a stickle begins; this grows to a water-slide; then comes a fallen tree through whose branches the stream washes and gurgles in muted tones. After that, once more there is the broad deep rumbling of the main current and all the repertoire is played over again, though never in the same order or with exact repetition of any part. Usually, too, more than one variety of stream-song is heard at the same moment. The string is double-stopped.

ODELL SHEPARD

Thy Rod and Thy Creel, incidentally, is dedicated to "Two good friends and good fishermen, loyal and devoted sons of Connecticut."

Myself, I never met Odell Shepard, to my sorrow; but *Thy Rod and Thy Creel* is one of the beckoning books in my limited library on fishing. It was Odell Shepard who said that "a good angler is likely to be a good man." Very true. It was he who put together one of the classic metaphors of the open field: "rooks rowing home to the elms with rust in their oar-locks."

And it was Ferris Greenslet who taught me what little I know about the fine art of dry fly fishing. I was with him on the upper Connecticut River in Colebrook when he, while running a small obliging fever, was working on a study of "The Fly-Rod in North America" for Hugh Sheringham and John C. Moore's magnificent—and magnificently illustrated—*Book of the Fly-Rod* (1931), published in London. Editor, scholar, Latinist, critic, biographer, fisherman, perfectionist, wit: Ferris Greenslet called his autobiography *Under The Bridge*; and this is the book from which our quotation is taken. When it was published by Houghton Mifflin Company on 9 November 1943, I wrote and sent him the following verse:

> My small, dry alder floating on the pool
> Reminds me that the grace of any art
> Is mastered only in that inward school
> Where self assigns to self the critic's part.
>
> And you who have with books and rivers made
> The prettiest alliance life can know
> Have said some things that, like the long cast laid
> Across the current, flash silver as they go.

HARTS BRIDGE,
WEST CORNWALL, CONNECTICUT

This covered bridge spanning the Housatonic River is some 212 feet long and well over 100 years old. It is one of the few remaining in Connecticut. It has survived a succession of floods and numerous severe ice jams. Along the banks of the river are delightful shady spots for picnics, and frequently there are fishermen wading in the shallow, turbulent river. Nearby is Kent Falls State Park, containing one of Connecticut's most spectacular waterfalls. The brook, arched by hemlocks, rushes over a precipice in two cascades, a 200-foot drop within a quarter of a mile. For this picture my hip boots were essential, for I had to wade well into the river.
Exposure—1/50 of a second at f:16. ASA Speed 50.

ARTHUR GRIFFIN

Uncomplicated Life

For most people who come from west of Buffalo or south of Washington, Vermont is doubtless too far away for a vacation home. Even for a New Yorker, all save the southern part of it is too far away for anyone who wants to spend all but his weekends in that interesting city whose symbol is a steel riveter, rampant. My farm is three hundred miles from New York; a brisk eight-hour drive: railroad connections abominable.

But for a writer, a teacher, a retired man of affairs, anyone who can take a two-month vacation, the place was appointed by the divine powers, and the only reason that I haven't gone into the Vermont real-estate business is that I have been somewhat occupied of late with sundry other forms of missionary labor.

For fifteen hundred to three thousand dollars, part down, you would, if you poked about long enough, find a hundred-acre farm with a solid old farmhouse of eight or ten rooms. It might have running water; it would not have a bathroom, electric lights, or a telephone. There would be one or two magnificently timbered old barns; one of them would make such a studio or minstrels' hall as to draw tears from Christopher Wren. It would be two-thirds of the way up a mountainside, protected from too shrewd a wind but looking ten or twenty miles down a valley between hills checkered with pastures among small forests of pine, maple, and poplar. With luck, it would have a trout stream. There would be one or two or three miles of dirt road, narrow, crooked, very decent in summer, foul in early spring and late autumn. Five

or ten miles away would be a village almost as gracious as Litchfield or Sharon. You can spend thirty dollars on modern improvements—i.e., fifteen for kerosene lamps and fifteen for a fine tin tank to bathe in—and have a stoutly comfortable place, an authentic home, for the rest of your life.

Your neighbors will be varied. Within a few miles of me, these past few years, have lived such slightly unco-ordinated persons, as George and Gilbert Seldes; Alexander Woollcott; Dr. Leo Wolman; Lynn Montross; Richard Billings, the great railroader; Fred Rothermell; Louis Adamic; and a gentleman named Calvin Coolidge. But, except at Dorset and Manchester, you will find no roar and flood of summerites. And as to the natives . . .

They are a complicated, reticent, slyly humorous lot, and I doubt if any place in the world will you find a citizenry which so strictly minds its own business. If you come to know them but slowly or not at all, they do not snoop; they do not pry; they have the reserve and self-respect of an ancient race that feels too secure to be more than just vaguely amused by the eccentricities of outlanders. Of a millionaire New Yorker, a Rodin, or a George Bernard Shaw, a Vermont farmer would stoutly say, "He ain't my kind of folks, but guess he's just as good as anybody else, long's he don't interfere with me."

It is a cool land, with ever-changing skies, this Vermont. For me it is peace and work and home.

SINCLAIR LEWIS

Sinclair Lewis died in Rome on 10 January 1951. The years of his Vermont farm—Twin Farms at South Pomfret—were 1929-1937. *The Man From Main Street*, edited by his literary executors, Harry E. Maule and Melville H. Cane, is a paperback selection of the essays and other writings by the author of *Main Street*: 1904-1950. The enormous range and vitality of these pieces open the great barn door to the freshness of new-mown hay.

As to the essay opposite, and apposite to, the present landscape: "They used to say of him [say the editors of *The Man From Main Street*] that 'Red is always buying places.' Certainly that was true of the last dozen years of his life. He bought and furnished no less than five homes, including the house in Bronxville, N.Y., Twin Farms at South Pomfret, Vermont, a big duplex apartment in New York, a Tudor castle in Duluth, and Thorvale Farm near Williamstown, Massachusetts, where he lived the last few years before his final trip to Italy. In that period he went abroad several times and stopped at innumerable New York hotels. This was, of course, a manifestation of his restlessness, his growing discontent with any one environment."

Robert Frost in his long life lived in a good many different houses in a good many different places and owned, at one time or another, a surprising diversity of property. We catch him on balance, as we do Sinclair Lewis, in the final six lines of the long poem called "New Hampshire":

I choose to be a plain New Hampshire farmer
With an income in cash of say a thousand
(From say a publisher in New York City).
It's restful to arrive at a decision,
And restful just to think about New Hampshire.
At present I am living in Vermont.

(Robert Frost)

LUDLOW, VERMONT

The mist-shrouded vista and haunting beauty of this pond is something few tourists see, or, when they are fortunate enough to see it, seldom bother to capture it on film. The pond actually is in the Black River, which connects and runs through the several Tyson Lakes. At the right of my view is a photogenic dam which maintains the water level of the lakes. This is on route 100, the Calvin Coolidge Highway. The ten miles from here to the Coolidge Homestead, now a National Shrine, abound with picture possibilities. I made this picture in early morning. Generally afternoon light is best.

Exposure—1/10 of a second at f:11. ASA Speed 50.

Upland Pastures

As you get up towards the Height of Land you come to what makes the returning New Englander draw breath quickly, the pleasure is so poignant: upland pastures dotted with juniper and boulders, and broken by clumps of balsam fir and spruce. Most fragrant, most beloved places. Dicksonia fern grows thick about the boulders. The pasturage is thin June-grass, the color of beach sand, as it ripens, and in August this is transformed to a queen's garden by the blossoming of blue asters and the little nemoralis golden-rod, which grew unnoticed all the earlier summer. Often whole stretches of the slope are carpeted with mayflowers and checkerberries, and as you climb higher, and meet the wind from the other side of the ridge, your foot crunches on gray reindeer-moss.

Last week, before climbing a small bare-peaked mountain, I turned aside to explore a path which led through a field of scattered balsam firs, with lady-fern growing thick about their feet. A little further on, the firs were assembled in groups and clumps, and then group was joined to group. The valley grew deeper and darker, and still the same small path led on, till I found myself in the tallest and most solemn wood of firs that I have ever seen. They were sixty feet high, needle-pointed, black, and they filled the long hollow between the hills, like a dark river.

The woods alternate with fields to clothe the hills and intervales and valleys, and make a constant and lovely variety over the landscape. Sometimes they seem a shore instead of a river. They jut out into the meadow-land, in capes and promontories, and stand in little islands, clustered around an outcropping ledge or a boulder too big to be removed. You are confronted everywhere with this meeting of the natural and indented shore of the woods, close, feathery, impenetrable, with the bays and inlets of field and pasture and meadow. The jutting portions are apt to be made more sharp and marked by the most striking part of our growth, the evergreens. There they grow, white pine and red pine, black spruce, hemlock, and balsam fir, in lovely sisterhood. Their needles shine in the sun. They taper perfectly, finished at every point, clean, dry, and resinous; and the fragrance distilled from them by our crystal air is as surely the very breath of New England as that of the Spice Islands is the breath of the East.

ROSALYND RICHARDS

Rosalynd Richards, daughter of a famous mother (Laura Richards) and granddaughter of Julia Ward Howe, is writing here of Maine. But East Orange touches on the same parallel as Wiscasset; and the spruce-look is clearly evident, as it is over in Coös County in New Hampshire. It is good for Maine and Vermont to visit each other now and then. Northern Maine, New Hampshire, or Vermont; how savory and strong is something in our memory awakened by those words, *upland pastures*.

Much as I love the grandeur of my western mountains, especially those of Oregon and Washington with which I was once familiar, I care mostly for the rolling hills of the more comfortable agrarian East. The only landscape I know which vaguely reminds me of Vermont is the southwest part of Pennsylvania where my ancestors finally dug in. But Vermont is really like no other state in the Union. In the north it has some memory of Scotland—especially in the bare-topped hills. But it is in the valleys of it, as here where Arthur Griffin set his sights, that I am most at home. Except for mountain trails, or driving through the gaps and gulfs, or beside Lake Champlain, the views in Vermont are rarely the long views—but they are satisfying. On a grander scale, the swelling Savannahs endless out of Omaha defend a certain disturbing beauty which comes with distance not too flat. All landscape, I am settled to believe, is tempered by other landscapes which we place within it or to which we extend it. Vermont, of all our states wherever, imposes no condition on this inner-outer reflex. It is Vermont in large part which led me once to conclude that New England is the authorized version of America.

142

EAST ORANGE, VERMONT

This village, off the beaten track, has one of the very few churches in Vermont that are not painted white. In middle September and October, the Vermont landscape glows briefly but radiantly. In this all-over scene you can observe where the scarlet, yellows, russets and oranges have replaced the summer greens. Soil, climate and trees combine to produce an annual foliage spectacle in Vermont. You will find many photogenic villages nearby, especially the Corinths, of which East Corinth is the best known.

Exposure—1/25 of a second at f:22. ASA Speed 50.

ARTHUR GRIFFIN

Enter Orion

THANKSGIVING PROCLAMATION

State of Connecticut
By His Excellency Wilbur L. Cross, Governor: a

PROCLAMATION

Time out of mind at this turn of the seasons when the hardy oak leaves rustle in the wind and the frost gives a tang to the air and the dusk falls early and the friendly evenings lengthen under the heel of Orion, it has seemed good to our people to join together in praising the Creator and Preserver, who has brought us by a way that we did not know to the end of another year. In observance of this custom, I appoint Thursday, the twenty-sixth of November, as a day of

PUBLIC THANKSGIVING

for the blessings that have been our common lot and have placed our beloved State with the favored regions of earth —for all the creature comforts: the yield of the soil that has fed us and the richer yield from labor of every kind that has sustained our lives—and for all those things, as dear as breath to the body, that quicken man's faith in his manhood, that nourish and strengthen his spirit to do the great work still before him: for the brotherly word and act; for honor held above price; for steadfast courage and zeal in the long, long search after truth; for liberty and for justice freely granted by each to his fellow and so as freely enjoyed; and for the crowning glory and mercy of peace upon our land—that we may humbly take heart of these blessings as we gather once again with solemn and festive rites to keep our Harvest Home.

12 November 1936   WILBUR L. CROSS

Nothing much can be done to a proclamation except to read it. Most proclamations cabbage a few worn words and crusty clichés, tie them together with a pumpkin rind, a bayonet, or fire cracker in due season, and there you are. Many appear ghostwritten for governors too occupied with split-level decisions of their own and others to do their homework.

Governor Wilbur L. Cross, scholar and long-time editor of *The Yale Review*, apparently enjoyed his proclamation deadlines. "For all those things, as dear as breath to the body . . ." This particular Thanksgiving outgiving, doubly signed by the Governor and by His Excellency's Command, seems to go with the soundless clash of symbols, the fall Connecticut scene, the old rail fence in particular. There is a groundswell in that prose opening: "Time out of mind at this turn of the seasons when the hardy oak leaves rustle in the wind . . ."

ജ ജ ജ ജ

But what of the day proclaimed? Dr. Cogswell of Windham, Connecticut (while still a youth), "undertook to officiate for his clergyman father who was too ill to hold the service" on Thanksgiving Day, 1788.

He perceived that nothing would be done without him and being "requested to proceed" he "pulled out his psalm book," and his hand trembled but very little. "Let us sing" said he, "the 97th Psalm," and he read it with a very audible voice. The music was fine; it entirely dissipated his timidities and as soon as it ceased, he arose and if he had had one on, he would probably have stroked his band; but as he had none, he wiped his face with his pocket handkerchief, named his text and went on. Some people would have called it reading; but really, he acted the preacher to admiration, as he was afterwards told by numbers of the congregation. The exercises were closed with an anthem from Isaiah, "Sing, O ye heavens, etc.," which was most enchantingly sung. After church, he repaired to his friend Devotion's and was treated with quite as much respect and attention as he desired. He drank flip, ate turkeys, pigs, pompion pies, apple pies, tarts, etc., etc., until he was perfectly satisfied. After supper he went home, gave thanks with his father, smoked a pipe for company's sake, bade the old folks good night, went into the kitchen, sung a number of songs to Polly and Betsey (his sisters), ate apples and nuts with them, and went to bed well satisfied with the transactions of the day.

(*Mason Fitch Cogswell*)

NORFOLK, CONNECTICUT

Norfolk is surrounded by many beautiful hills, including Ball Mountain and Haystack Mountain. It is tucked away in the northwest corner of Connecticut, less than five miles from the Massachusetts border. The flat stone walls and the split rail fences of the Nutmeg State have given me pictures quite different from other states. Emerson said, "He was a first rate neighbor and he always kept his fences up." I'm happy about those fences.

Exposure—1/25 of a second at f:16. ASA Speed 50.

ARTHUR GRIFFIN

Farewell, Thou Busy World!

In more open brook fishing it is always a fascinating problem to decide how to fish a favorite pool or ripple, for much depends upon the hour of the day, the light, the height of water, the precise period of the spring or summer. But after one has decided upon the best theoretical procedure, how often the stupid trout prefers some other plan. And when you have missed a fish that you counted upon landing, what solid satisfaction is still possible for you, if you are philosopher enough to sit down then and there, eat your lunch, smoke a meditative pipe, and devise a new campaign against that particular fish. To get another rise from him after lunch is a triumph of diplomacy; to land him is nothing short of statesmanship. For sometimes he will jump furiously at a fly for very devilishness without ever meaning to take it, and then, wearying suddenly of his gymnastics, he will snatch sulkily at a grasshopper, beetle, or worm. Trout feed upon an extraordinary variety of crawling things, as all fishermen know who practice the useful habit of opening the first two or three fish they catch, to see what food is that day the favorite. But here, as elsewhere in this world, the best things lie nearest, and there is no bait so killing, week in and week out, as your plain garden or golf-green angleworm.

Walton's list of possible worms is impressive, and his directions for placing them upon the hook have the placid completeness that belonged to his character. Yet in such matters a little nonconformity may be encouraged. No two men or boys dig bait in quite the same way, though all share, no doubt, the singular elation which gilds that grimy occupation with the spirit of romance. Nor do any two experienced fishermen hold quite the same theory as to the best mode of baiting the hook. There are a hundred ways, each of them good.

As to the best hook for worm fishing . . . Whose rods are best for bait fishing . . . Such questions, like those pertaining to the boots or coat which one should wear, the style of bait box one should carry, or the brand of tobacco best suited for smoking in the wind, are topics for unending discussion among the serious minded around the campfire. . . . They are counsels of worldly wisdom, but they leave the soul untouched. A man may have them at his fingers' ends and be no better fisherman at bottom; or he may . . . ignore most of the admitted rules and come home with a full basket. It is a sufficient defense of fishing with a worm to pronounce the truism that no man is a *complete* angler until he has mastered all the modes of angling. Lovely streams, lonely and enticing but impossible to fish with a fly, await the fisherman who is not too proud to use, with a man's skill, the same unpretentious tackle which he began with as a boy.

BLISS PERRY

Although I have joyfully fished with a fly since my boyhood days on the far-off Rogue River in Oregon, I somehow suspect the *absolute* purist who has never fished with a worm, as I somehow suspect the legion of lesser figures in the wake of Picasso and Matisse who have small knowledge of the art of drawing. Fishing with a worm is first principle: an art in itself.

Bliss Perry, whose favored Lemoille is in northern Vermont where I have looked for trout myself, is writing of the Taylor Brook; but the pools in the fine picture east of you would have interested him; and to the fly-trap overhang he would not have given a second thought. To this great Emersonian, every word indeed was once a poem. Bliss Perry's speech had deep sonorities and the rhythm in it of the wash of waters. He talked the way he fished; and though I never followed him down stream or up, I have no doubt that his calm action on the brook or in the river was as skillful as a line of Sapphics, forthright as a flick of old John Skelton.

WELLS RIVER, GROTON, VERMONT

At any season Vermont abounds in beautiful pictures, but autumn with its blazing palette is the most spectacular of all. I'm always amazed to find, away up in the hills, on the highways and at some of my favorite locations, photographers from the far West and most every other section of the country who journey to New England for our annual color show. The proper timing is very important, so that you will be in the most colorful area every day. Usually I start up north and work south, hoping that a sudden wind and heavy rain doesn't come up to strip the trees. These little falls are just a few feet off route 302 about a mile west of Groton. Lake Groton, the source of the Wells River, is only four miles away. Unless you like backlighting, early morning light is best.

Exposure—1/25 of a second at f:14. ASA Speed 50.

ARTHUR GRIFFIN

WINTER

Unto the Hills

There is a sensation of soul in the spiritual desires of one that loves God, which is entirely different from all natural desires: both spiritual love and natural love are attended with delight in the object beloved; but the sensations of delight are not the same, but entirely and exceedingly diverse. Natural men may have conceptions of many things about spiritual affections; but there is something in them which is as it were the nucleus, or kernel of them, that they have no more conception of, than one born blind has of colours.

JONATHAN EDWARDS

Christianity arose among Galilean peasants who were never responsible for maintaining a social system. Its precepts are personal. It arose amongst a people devoid of the plastic arts. These were, in fact, forbidden by their traditional religion. It arose amongst a people devoid of science. That, too, would have been forbidden had they known what it was. It arose amongst a pastoral people with next to no technology, yet its mandates have lingered on into an age dominated by the impact of novel scientific techniques. This conflict, this dichotomy in our spiritual life, is felt by multitudes who do not know what it means and many of whom are scandalized or terrified when its meaning is pointed out

to them. I cite you the experience of ancient Hellas because the Greeks are the only people in the western world who ever created from the ground up a culture on the grand scale, who ever faced with candor the problems incurred in so doing, and bequeathed to us a heritage of thought and experience which may see us through our own ordeal.

LUCIEN PRICE

I do not know what is true. I do not know the meaning of the universe. But in the midst of doubt, in the collapse of creeds, there is one thing I do not doubt, that no man who lives in the same world with most of us can doubt, and that is that the faith is true and adorable which leads a soldier to throw away his life in obedience to a blindly accepted duty, in a cause which he little understands, in a plan of campaign of which he has no notion, under tactics of which he does not see the use. . . .

It is enough for us that the universe has produced us and has within it, as less than it, all that we believe and love. If we think of our existence not as that of a little god outside, but as that of a ganglion within, we have the infinite behind us. It gives us our only but our adequate significance.

OLIVER WENDELL HOLMES, JR.

Lucien Price was a highly civilized man: editorial writer for the Boston *Globe*, a Greek enthusiast, student of music and literature, admirer of Alfred North Whitehead, and an authority on Sibelius. The selected words are from "Amphion's Lyre," an address to the Harvard Glee Club, 31 May 1945.

Oliver Wendell Holmes, Jr., wrote the first part of his quoted Credo seventy-one years ago. The second paragraph (part of a longer one) was written in 1918. They came to me by way of *A Commonplace Book* by Charles P. Curtis. The 1895 words are from a speech which Justice Holmes gave at Harvard on Memorial Day, 1895, called "A Soldier's Faith." The other half is from the end of an article called "Natural Law" in the *Collected Legal Papers*.

It is only a step from the trilogy of Holmes, Price, and Edwards to Calvin Coolidge and his testament of faith in the State of Vermont. Speaking from a train platform in Bennington in 1928, President Coolidge said:

I love Vermont because of her hills and valleys, her scenery and invigorating climate, but most of all because of her indomitable people. They are a race of pioneers who have almost beggared themselves to serve others. If the spirit of liberty should vanish in other parts of our Union and support of our institutions should languish, it could all be replenished from the generous store held by the people of this brave little State of Vermont.

(Calvin Coolidge)

GRAFTON, VERMONT

*This peaceful, small settlement off the beaten track
in southern Vermont sees little traffic. In summer
it is very quiet—in the winter even more so. Don't
expect to find the conditions as perfect as I did
after a new snowstorm, but the church is always
there. I had this type of picture in mind for years,
but had to wait for the right combination of snow
and lighting, with of course the ideal subject.
Afternoon light is best. I was very happy to have
David McCord select Lucien Price's "Amphion's
Lyre" for one of his paragraphs to introduce my
favorite church in Vermont. I worked with Lucien
for many years on the Boston* Globe. *He loved
New England, especially Vermont.*

Exposure—1/25 of a second at f:20. ASA Speed 50.

Into the Wind

The most foreign and picturesque structures on the Cape, to an inlander, not excepting the salt-works, are the wind-mills,—gray-looking, octagonal towers, with long timbers slanting to the ground in the rear, and there resting on a cart-wheel, by which their fans are turned round to face the wind. These appeared also to serve in some measure for props against its force. A great circular rut was worn around the building by the wheel. The neighbors who assemble to turn the mill to the wind are likely to know which way it blows, without a weather-cock. They looked loose and slightly locomotive, like huge wounded birds, trailing a wing or a leg, and reminded one of pictures of the Netherlands. Being on elevated ground, and high in themselves, they serve as landmarks,—for there are no tall trees, or other objects commonly, which can be seen at a distance in the horizon; though the outline of the land itself is so firm and distinct, that an insignificant cone, or even precipice of sand, is visible at a great distance from over the sea. Sailors making the land commonly steer either by the windmills, or the meeting-houses. In the country, we are obliged to steer by the meeting-houses alone. Yet the meeting-house is a kind of windmill, which runs one day in seven, turned either by the winds of doctrine or public opinion, or more rarely by the winds of Heaven, where another sort of grist is ground, of which, if it be not all bran or musty, if it be not *plaster*, we trust to make bread of life.

HENRY DAVID THOREAU

As one who loved ocean beaches, gulls wheeling in the sky, dunes baking in the sun, gleaming surf and salt spray, he was particularly pleased to establish three national sea-shores, above all the one covering white beaches and serene inland ponds of his own Cape Cod.

ARTHUR M. SCHLESINGER, JR.
[On President John F. Kennedy]

159

Windmill, West Harwich, Cape Cod: Winter. The scene is just ninety-six years away from Thoreau and about one-tenth of that in miles from the Kennedy compound.

In *The Small Years*, a book of childhood "in love with life in the few years that closed the nineteenth century," Frank Kendon speaks of "the look of everlastingness." It is a phrase to remember as I have remembered it for thirty-five years. In *A Thousand Days*, from which Mr. Schlesinger's comment is drawn, there are these words from the late President's address (March, 1961) dedicating the National Wildlife Federation Building: "He [President Kennedy] affirmed the responsibility 'to hand down undiminished to those who come after us, as was handed down by those who went before, the natural wealth and beauty which is ours.'" All conservationists should get by heart this codicil from Henry Beston: "Do no dishonour to the earth lest you dishonour the spirit of man."

HERRING RIVER, WEST HARWICH, MASSACHUSETTS

The enchantment of Cape Cod in winter is something you just cannot believe if you see the Cape only in the rush of summer. To get a picture of this type you either have to live on the Cape or drive down directly after an unusually heavy snow, for the Cape doesn't get many lasting snows. (Some of my friends golf most every day of the year on the Cape.) Last winter we spent four days after a good storm, but because of poor light took only two pictures.

Exposure—1/50 of a second at f:16. ASA Speed 50.

ARTHUR GRIFFIN

19 April 1775

After I had been there [Lexington] about half an hour, Mr. Dawes came; we refreshed ourselves, and set off for Concord. We were overtaken by a young Dr. Prescott, whom we found to be a high Son of Liberty. . . .

We had got nearly half way. Mr. Dawes and the doctor stopped to alarm the people of a house. I was about one hundred rods ahead when I saw two men in nearly the same situation as those officers were near Charlestown. I called for the doctor and Mr. Dawes to come up. In an instant I was surrounded by four. They had placed themselves in a straight road that inclined each way; they had taken down a pair of bars on the north side of the road, and two of them were under a tree in the pasture. The doctor being foremost, he came up and we tried to get past them; but they being armed with pistols and swords, they forced us into the pasture. The doctor jumped his horse over a low stone wall and got to Concord.

I observed a wood at a small distance and made for that. When I got there, out started six officers on horseback and ordered me to dismount. One of them, who appeared to have the command, examined me, where I came from and what my name was. I told him. He asked me if I was an express. I answered in the affirmative. He demanded what time I left Boston. I told him, and added that their troops had catched aground in passing the river, and that there would be five hundred Americans there in a short time, for I had alarmed the country all the way up. He immediately rode towards those who stopped us, when all five of them came down upon a full gallop. One of them, whom I afterwards found to be a Major Mitchel, of the 5th Regiment, clapped his pistol to my head, called me by name and told me he was going to ask me some questions, and if I did not give him true answers, he would blow my brains out. He then asked me similar questions to those above. He then ordered me to mount my horse, after searching me for arms. He then ordered them to advance and to lead me in front. When we got to the road, they turned down towards Lexington. When we had got about one mile, the major rode up to the officer that was leading me, and told him to give me to the sergeant. As soon as he took me, the major ordered him, if I attempted to run, or anybody insulted them, to blow my brains out.

We rode till we got near Lexington meeting-house, when the militia fired a volley of guns, which appeared to alarm them very much. The major inquired of me how far it was to Cambridge, and if there were any other road. After some consultation, the major rode up to the sergeant and asked if his horse was tired. He answered him he was—he was a sergeant of grenadiers and had a small horse. "Then," said he, "take that man's horse." I dismounted, and the sergeant mounted my horse, when they all rode towards Lexington meeting-house.

PAUL REVERE

Thus Paul Revere. And thus the familiar Minute Man, reminding us that we are now but a few years short of the two hundredth anniversary of the Battle of Lexington. At two o'clock on that morning of 19 April 1775, as the silversmith-patriot reached the bridge in Concord Town, "Lexington common was alive with minutemen; and not with them only, but with the old men, who were exempts, except in case of immediate danger to the town." Thus George Bancroft, the historian of that sad business on the famous green now visited by tourists in their thousands every year:

Jonas Parker, the strongest and best wrestler in Lexington, had promised never to run from British troops; and he kept his vow. A wound brought him on his knees. Having discharged his gun, he was preparing to load it again, when he was stabbed by a bayonet, and lay on the post which he took at the morning's drum-beat. So fell Isaac Muzzey, and so died the aged Robert Munroe, who in 1758 had been an ensign at Louisburg. Jonathan Harrington, junior, was struck in front of his own house on the north of the common. His wife was at the window as he fell. With blood gushing from his breast, he rose in her sight, tottered, fell again, then crawled on hands and knees toward his dwelling; she ran to meet him, but only reached him as he expired on their threshold. Caleb Harrington, who had gone into the meeting-house for powder, was shot as he came out. Samuel Hadley and John Brown were pursued, and killed after they had left the green. Asahel Porter, of Woburn, who had been taken prisoner by the British on the march, endeavoring to escape, was shot within a few rods of the common. Seven men of Lexington were killed, nine wounded; a quarter part of all who stood in arms on the green.

Day came in all the beauty of an early spring. The trees were budding; the grass growing rankly a full month before its time; the blue-bird and the robin gladdening the genial season, and calling forth the beams of the sun which on that morning shone with the warmth of summer; but distress and horror gathered over the inhabitants of the peaceful town. There on the green lay in death the gray-haired and the young; the grassy field was red "with the innocent blood of their brethren slain," crying unto God for vengeance from the ground.

(George Bancroft)

LEXINGTON, MASSACHUSETTS

Standing on one corner of the triangular Lexington Green is the arresting statue of Captain John Parker (a friend of mine was the model for this statue). It was here, on April 19, 1775, that local farmers gathered to resist the British troops and fought the first battle of the American Revolution. The Buckman Tavern was the headquarters of the Colonists and they had assembled in the early morning when they heard that the Redcoats were coming. This is a popular tourist spot. Shortly after I made this picture a couple of school buses arrived and almost all the children had cameras.

Exposure—1/50 of a second at f:20. ASA Speed 50.

ARTHUR GRIFFIN

No Taste for Trifles

A natural skill for mensuration, growing out of his mathematical knowledge and his habit of ascertaining the measures and distances of objects which interested him, the size of trees, the depth and extent of ponds and rivers, the height of mountains and the air-line distance of his favorite summits—this, and his intimate knowledge of the territory about Concord, made him drift into the profession of land-surveyor. It had the advantage for him that it led him continually into new and secluded grounds, and helped his studies of Nature. His accuracy and skill in this work were readily appreciated, and he found all the employment he wanted.

He could easily solve the problems of the surveyor, but he was daily beset with graver questions, which he manfully confronted. He interrogated every custom, and wished to settle all his practice on an ideal foundation. He was a protestant *à outrance*, and few lives contain so many renunciations. He was bred to no profession; he never married; he lived alone; he never went to church; he never voted; he refused to pay a tax to the State; he ate no flesh, he drank no wine, he never knew the use of tobacco; and, though a naturalist, he used neither trap nor gun. He chose, wisely no doubt for himself, to be the bachelor of thought and Nature. He had no talent for wealth, and knew how to be poor without the least hint of squalor or inelegance. . . . "I am often reminded," he wrote in his journal, "that if I had bestowed on me the wealth of Croesus, my aims must be still the same, and my means essentially the same." He had no temptations to fight against—no appetites, no passions, no taste for elegant trifles. A fine house, dress, the manners and talk of highly cultivated people were all thrown away on him. He much preferred a good Indian, and considered these refinements as impediments to conversation, wishing to meet his companion on the simplest terms. . . . When asked at table what dish he preferred, he answered, "The nearest."

He chose to be rich by making his wants few, and supplying them himself. . . . There was somewhat military in his nature, not to be subdued, always manly and able, but rarely tender, as if he did not feel himself except in opposition. He wanted a fallacy to expose, a blunder to pillory, I may say required a little sense of victory, a roll of the drum, to call his powers into full exercise. It cost him nothing to say No; indeed he found it much easier than to say Yes. It seemed as if his first instinct on hearing a proposition was to controvert it, so impatient was he of the limitations of our daily thought. This habit, of course, is a little chilling to the social affections; and though the companion would in the end acquit him of any malice or untruth, yet it mars conversation. Hence, no equal companion stood in affectionate relations with one so pure and guileless. "I love Henry," said one of his friends, "but I cannot like him; and as for taking his arm, I should as soon think of taking the arm of an elm-tree."

RALPH WALDO EMERSON *On Thoreau*

If Henry was never really out of the sound of Mrs. Emerson's dinner bell, one may doubt that his rambles took him often so far to the west of Concord as Groton; but the setting and the woods in the study opposite are as typical of outlying Concord as they are of the other. And that elm tree, on which the previous passage closes, looms there eloquent in silhouette: indeed, one may choose between several.

And if this landscape and a touch of masterly prose should lead one curious reader back to Emerson's funeral address on his younger friend as it was printed in *The Atlantic Monthly* in 1862, this book will not have been printed in vain. Few eulogies in the world of letters are the equal of what Emerson said in honor of Thoreau. This is the essay which rises again and again to the heights of Thoreau's *Walden* and "his mythical record of his [own] disappointments":

I long ago lost a hound, a bay horse and a turtle-dove, and am still on their trail. Many are the travellers I have spoken concerning them, describing their tracks, and what calls they answered to. I have met one or two who have heard the hound, and the tramp of the horse, and even seen the dove disappear behind a cloud; and they seemed as anxious to recover them as if they had lost them themselves.

(Henry David Thoreau)

GROTON, MASSACHUSETTS

My neighbors often wonder if I'm sane when I welcome each new snowstorm with glee. Overnight, everything is changed. High drifts erase ugly landscapes, and trees laden with freshly fallen snow take on new beauty. I have found that the most dramatic snow pictures are made in the very late afternoon. It is then that you can get those beautiful blue and purple shadows. I had just about enough time to get the tripod and camera out of the car before the sun went down on this study. It is an old mill pond about a mile east of the town. Very low cross lighting makes this picture, with the tall marsh grass almost touching the lens. The pattern of the snow and the spotting of the sunlight carry the eye into the distance.

Exposure—1/10 of a second at f:32. ASA Speed 50.

ARTHUR GRIFFIN

Snowbound

All day the gusty north-wind bore
The loosening drift its breath before;
Low circling round its southern zone,
The sun through dazzling snow-mist shone.
No church-bell lent its Christian tone
To the savage air, no social smoke
Curled over woods of snow-hung oak.
A solitude made more intense
By dreary-voicéd elements,
The shrieking of the mindless wind,
The moaning tree-boughs swaying blind,
And on the glass the unmeaning beat
Of ghostly finger-tips of sleet.
Beyond the circle of our hearth
No welcome sound of toil or mirth
Unbound the spell, and testified
Of human life and thought outside.
We minded that the sharpest ear
The buried brooklet could not hear,
The music of whose liquid lip
Had been to us companionship,
And, in our lonely life, had grown
To have an almost human tone.

As night drew on, and, from the crest
Of wooded knolls that ridged the west,

The sun, a snow-blown traveller, sank
From sight beneath the smothering bank,
We piled, with care, our nightly stack
Of wood against the chimney-back,—
The oaken log, green, huge, and thick,
And on its top the stout back-stick;
The knotty forestick laid apart,
And filled between with curious art
The ragged brush; then, hovering near,
We watched the first red blaze appear,
Heard the sharp crackle, caught the gleam
On whitewashed wall and sagging beam,
Until the old, rude-furnished room
Burst, flower-like, into rosy bloom;
While radiant with a mimic flame
Outside the sparkling drift became,
And through the bare-boughed lilac-tree
Our own warm hearth seemed blazing free.
The crane and pendent trammels showed,
The Turks' heads on the andirons glowed;
While childish fancy, prompt to tell
The meaning of the miracle,
Whispered the old rhyme: "*Under the tree*,
When fire outdoors burns merrily,
There the witches are making tea."

JOHN GREENLEAF WHITTIER

"The pioneers carried Whittier with them," says Van Wyck Brooks, "as emigrant Scotsmen carried the poems of Burns. *Snow Bound* was their image of Pallas, the safeguard of their memories. It was the touchstone of their past." John Ciardi calls *Snowbound* a native idyll, in which "the richness of a native feeling emerges whole and unself-conscious."

But no one can do justice to New England weather—justice in words, that is—without some reference to Thoreau. He runs a fine Bach counterpoint to Whittier's Schumann. Here is a paragraph from "A Winter Walk":

The wonderful purity of nature at this season is a most pleasing fact. Every decayed stump and moss-grown stone and rail, and the dead leaves of autumn, are concealed by a clean napkin of snow. In the bare fields and tinkling woods, see what virtue survives. In the coldest and bleakest places, the warmest charities still maintain a foothold. A cold and searching wind drives away all contagion, and nothing can withstand it but what has a virtue in it, and accordingly, whatever we meet with in cold and bleak places, as the tops of mountains, we respect for a sort of sturdy innocence, a Puritan toughness. All things beside seem to be called in for shelter, and what stays out must be part of the original frame of the universe, and of such valor as God himself. It is invigorating to breathe the cleansed air. Its greater fineness and purity are visible to the eye, and we would fain stay out long and late, that the gales may sigh through us, too, as through the leafless trees, and fit us for the winter,—as if we hoped so to borrow some pure and steadfast virtue, which will stead us in all seasons.

(Henry David Thoreau)

172

GOSHEN, CONNECTICUT

Many think of manufacturing and insurance as the important resources of Connecticut, but it has also a surprising variety of scenery. Each of the seasons has a special flavor. The town of Goshen is not now well known. In pre-Civil War days, John Brown, the abolitionist, made a dramatic raid on the U.S. Arsenal at Harper's Ferry which brought the town renown. Nearby is his birthplace, and only a few miles beyond on a high plateau above the Naugatuck Valley looms the stately old town of Litchfield (which I had in my first all-color book, New England*). I had many other snow pictures in mind for this page, but this cold scene has significance for me because it won an award in a World Wide Photo Contest.*

Exposure—1/25 of a second at f:22. ASA Speed 50.

ARTHUR GRIFFIN

Two Rivers

Thy summer voice, Musketaquit,
Repeats the music of the rain;
But sweeter rivers pulsing flit
Through thee, as thou through Concord Plain.

Thou in thy narrow banks are pent:
The stream I love unbounded goes
Through flood and sea and firmament;
Through light, through life, it forward flows.

I see the inundation sweet,
I hear the spending of the stream
Through years, through men, through Nature fleet,
Through love and thought, through power and dream.

Musketaquit, a goblin strong,
Of shard and flint makes jewels gay;
They lose their grief who hear his song,
And where he winds is the day of day.

So forth and brighter fares my stream—
Who drink it shall not thirst again;
No darkness stains its equal gleam,
And ages drop in it like rain.

RALPH WALDO EMERSON

Emerson's poem is called "Two Rivers"; sometimes "The Two Rivers." The two rivers in question are the Sudbury and the Assabet at Concord. Arthur Griffin's tripod stood not many rods below the confluence. I find this poem of Emerson strangely absent from most of the anthologies. Of course the Brahma turn of phrase and line combine to make it an exquisite study in how a poem persuasive, still perversely manages to mean. "The little Musketaquid also," says Odell Shepard of the river—"the little Musketaquid also, that steals through Concord with so slow a tread that Hawthorne was for three weeks in doubt which way it flows, has nothing to learn in the lore of rivers." Musketaquit—I cross back to the Emersonian 't'—is not really a river but the long marshy stretch of the Sudbury as it winds round upper Concord. The Indian word means Prairie River. Emerson's second river, of course, is that which flows "through flood and sea and firmament." As Louis Untermeyer says, "The suavity of Emerson's verse is deceptive. The surface is so limpid, so easily persuasive, that it appears conventional."

It is but a long stone's throw from these gathered geese to the Old Manse, built in 1765 "by the warlike minister, William Emerson, who from its grounds watched the fight." Hawthorne, as his second most famous book suggests by its title alone, lived here from 1842 to 1845. It was here also that Ralph Waldo Emerson wrote the essay "Nature," quoted from on page 33. Van Wyck Brooks gives a weirdly memorable picture of a small skating party on the river, beginning likely at this precise point.

The music-box at the Manse belonged to Thoreau, Henry David Thoreau, the pencil-maker, Emerson's *protégé*, who had gone to Staten Island for a visit, to tutor the children of Emerson's brother William. It was a gift of Margaret Fuller's brother to the youthful poet-naturalist who, as one of his friends said, was "getting up a nose like Emerson's." Hawthorne had skated with him on the river, wrapped in his long cloak, and marvelled at Thoreau's dithyrambic dances and Dionysian leaps over the ice, while Emerson pitched along in the weary rear. Hawthorne had bought from Thoreau the fisherman's dory, green with a border of blue, the "Musketaquid," in which Henry and his brother had spent a week on the Concord and Merrimac rivers. Thoreau had changed his name. Dr. Ripley had christened him David Henry, and he had reversed these appellations, after the Concord fashion. For Emerson had altered the name of his wife from Lydia to Lidian, Alcott had revised his native Alcox, and Hawthorne, years before, had inserted the w in his father's "Hathorne." This practice of the Concord authors symbolized their love of independence and, better still, their love of euphony; for all these Concordians were Pythagoreans, and the followers of Pythagoras have a taste for pleasing and musical names.

(*Van Wyck Brooks*)

176

CONCORD RIVER, CONCORD, MASSACHUSETTS

Since my home in Winchester is close to Concord I have photographed this area time after time, but had never seen so many wild Canada Geese there before I made this picture. I was driving over the Lowell Road bridge on a very dull afternoon when I first saw the geese. Using a telephoto lens so I wouldn't disturb the visitors, I made one exposure and then waited almost an hour for better light. Around the bend in the background stands the historic Rude Bridge that Arched the Flood.

Exposure—1/25 of a second with a 15-inch lens at f:16. ASA Speed 50.

ARTHUR GRIFFIN

Beyond the Lights

Of a frosty November night one sees the glow in the windows of the farmhouse that speaks of an atmosphere within, a tranquil social time, a gathering for some ease after the strain of the day's work, for shelter, comfort, repose. And yet the same cold moonlight that glimmers on the roof sees a dark something stir in the close shrubs and grasses of the swamp, something that seems to imply an abortive activity, to writhe, but without progress.

It is the struggle between the insensate trap and the mink, fox, or raccoon on whose flesh its fangs are set. Either exhaustion follows, and subsequent death at the hands of the trapper—who will visit the spot at dawn, or two or three days hence—or an escape by means compared with which the sacrifice of Scaevola's right hand was a slight essay of stoicism. Then, in a dreadfully imposed silence, the captive creature with its sharp teeth desperately rends its own flesh, and even gnaws and crushes its own bones—and is free.

Such tragedies transpire in the darkness of wood and swamp, unrecorded, unheeded. Scaevola won the approbation of all succeeding time that he suffered the deprivation of his hand as a pledge of fidelity to his principles; but I never heard it recorded as a heroism in mink or raccoon that with his own teeth he severed flesh and sinew because he loved freedom and his natural rights. Indeed, the scientific have averred that in such cases of voluntary dismemberment the suffering is slight.

Of those who speak thus lightly of pain and wrong, soothing the disturbed and doubting conscience and giving countenance to the evil . . . they are paid in such coin as those thirty pieces, of which a man's strength could not endure the weight, heavy with innocent blood.

EDWARD MARTIN TABER

Edward Martin Taber was born on Staten Island in 1863 and died in Washington, Connecticut, in 1896. In 1887, "exiled from New York, as his only chance for life," he chose to live in Stowe, Vermont. He was a pupil of Abbott H. Thayer who wrote the introduction to *Stowe Notes*, a leisurely Taber volume rich in journal entries, letters, and (above all) some first-rate reproductions of his drawings and exquisite paintings of the Vermont landscape. No one, to my knowledge, ever put Vermont in oils with such delicate balance, firmness, and flawless sense of values.

A compassionate amateur naturalist, Taber's words on the trapping of animals reminds me of this other (and much more remarkable) passage by Henry Beston, author of *The Outermost House*, from which book it is taken:

> We need another and a wiser and perhaps a more mystical concept of animals. Remote from universal nature, and living by complicated artifice, man in civilization surveys the creature through the glass of his knowledge and sees thereby a feather magnified and the whole image in distortion. We patronize them for their incompleteness, for their tragic fate of having taken form so far below ourselves. And therein we err, and greatly err. For the animal shall not be measured by man. In a world older and more complete than ours they move finished and complete, gifted with extensions of the senses we have lost or never attained, living by voices we shall never hear. They are not brethren, they are not underlings; they are other nations, caught with ourselves in the net of life and time, fellow prisoners of the splendour and travail of the earth.

> *(Henry Beston)*

LOWER WATERFORD, VERMONT

This small settlement is called "The White Village." The dozen or so buildings, with the exception of the post office, are painted white. The late afternoon we arrived here conditions were good. There was a strong blue sky, so my wife and I went to all the homes and the Inn and had them turn on lights in all rooms facing my camera position. We got the keys for the church, to illuminate that, and then waited on the hill for dusk, meanwhile almost freezing. The most colorful night pictures are taken at dusk. It has to be dark enough to have the lights show and at the same time have the sky blue. Five minutes after taking this picture the sky would photograph black. The lights behind the church steeple are of the Moore Dam that is on the Connecticut River which is the border of Vermont and New Hampshire. Note that the blue snow is not a mistake. Snow is that color at that time of day because the blue sky light is its only illumination.

Exposure—about 20 seconds at f:16. Ektachrome Daylight film. ASA Speed 50.

ARTHUR GRIFFIN

Hieroglyphics

It is very unusual for the dunes to be held down by such an unbroken coating of snow and ice, that the blowing of the sand ceases and dune growth and change are stilled. This state of affairs occurred, however, in the winter of 1919–20. The earlier snowstorms of the winter were heavy and wet; the snow fell quietly, coating the sand thickly and freezing into a solid sheet. Later storms added to the accumulation and the dry surface snow blew about and formed drifts that were, for the most part, spotless white and free from contamination with the darker sand which was held prisoner below. Winter is generally the season of greatest movement in the dunes, for the winds are then the strongest and, as a rule, the snow and sand blow about together, forming gray drifts of mingled sand and snow. In the northern blasts, the conical dunes smoke at the top like wigwams, the cirque dunes are rapidly undercut and build up to leeward and the desert dunes deposit their load of snow and sand on the steep southern side. Often the snow and sand are segregated and form alternate layers, wavy lines and concentric circles, alternately gray and white, sometimes in patterns of considerable beauty.

On one occasion I was following the tracks of a white-footed mouse. These were joined by those of a fox. There were some irregular jumps on the part of the fox and the mouse tracks vanished. Again I found the body of a herring gull on the beach with head torn off and much of the flesh gone. It was surrounded by tracks of both fox and crow, but I venture to affirm that these two were not companions at the feast.

A dead creature on the beach always attracts the scavengers. A big loon thrown up at the top of the tide was surrounded by tracks in which those of crow, fox and skunk could easily be recognized. The skunk had ambled up in the night from low water and was making for the dunes twenty feet to leeward of the loon; suddenly he stopped, "skidding" a little, turned at right angles and trotted directly to the loon. The loon was recently dead, a wounded bird, no doubt, that had escaped the clutches of the gunner. It showed no mark of tooth or claw, but had been inspected only, and left until it was more tender eating. The fox had kicked up sand over it and there was the mark of his foot in the sand on the loon's back.

CHARLES WENDELL TOWNSEND

It is not many miles as the crow flies—and a great many crows are continually flying, beachcombing, resting, fighting, feeding, and talking in the leisurely, accurate, perceptive, and delightful essays of this medical-naturalist;—it is not many miles as the crow flies from the present site of the camera lens to the dunes, marshes, and pine islands of Dr. Townsend's Ipswich region. And well within gull range lie "The Dry Salvages," the subject of one of Eliot's *Four Quartets*. *Salvages*, he is quick to tell you, rhymes with *assuages*.

Among the many charms of Dr. Townsend's *Sand Dunes and Salt Marshes* (1913) and *Beach Grass* (1923) are his astonishing photographic studies of tracks in the sand: birds, animals, bugs, toads, caterpillars—everything but man. Both books, alas, to my uncertain knowledge, are out of print. Eliot, of course, is not. It was my friend Walter Muir Whitehill, Director of the Boston Athenaeum, who put me on the track of Dr. Townsend.

WINGAERSHEEK BEACH, WEST GLOUCESTER, MASSACHUSETTS

I'm always surprised by the very few tourists and camera fans you see on Cape Ann in the winter. Gloucester, Rockport and the small settlements are just as photogenic in the winter as in the summer. Usually seen in summer garb, when it is one of the most popular of beaches, here is Wingaersheek in the bleak cold of winter, with a frosting of snow. Beyond is Annisquam across the Annisquam river. I made this on a very windy, cold late afternoon, with the temperature approaching zero. I just managed to get the picture before the shutter of my camera and my fingers froze.

Exposure—1/50 of a second at f:14. ASA Speed 50.

184

ARTHUR GRIFFIN

Toward Oregon

Nevertheless, when all these reasons are totaled up they make a sum far from large enough to explain why, suddenly, the Americans were marching on their last frontier —to explain the evening talk in farm kitchens in January, 1846. One comes much closer to the truth with Boone and Carver and Gist, with the venturers crossing the fixed frontier of Sudbury toward the new land in the Connecticut bottoms—with all those who in two and a quarter centuries had moved up to the Fall Line and beyond it, across to the Mississippi, and, a few years since, beyond that. . . . When Bill Bowen sold his house a national emotion welled in the secret places of his heart and he joined himself to a national myth. He believed with Henry Thoreau in the forest and in the meadow and in the night in which the corn grows. Eastward Thoreau went only by force, but westward, ever since Columbus dared the Ocean Sea, westward he had gone free. The lodestone of the West tugged deep in the blood, as deep as desire. When the body dies, the Book of the Dead relates, the soul is borne along the pathway of the setting sun. Toward that Western horizon all heroes of all peoples known to history have always traveled. Beyond it have lain all the Fortunate Isles that literature knows. Beyond the Gates of Hercules, beyond the Western Ocean, beyond the peaks where the sun sinks, the Lapps and the Irish and the Winnebago and all others have known that they would find the happy Hyperboreans—the open country, freedom, the unknown. Westward lies the goal of effort. And, if either Freud or the Navajo speak true, westward we shall find the hole in the earth through which the soul may plunge to peace.

BERNARD DeVOTO

To this may be added a quotation from Bernard DeVoto's *New England: There She Stands.*

"New England is a finished place. Its destiny is that of Florence or Venice, not Milan, while the American empire careens onward toward its unpredicted end. . . . It is the first American section to be finished, to achieve stability in the conditions of its life. It is the first old civilization, the first permanent civilization in America."

Bernard DeVoto, vigorous New England implant from the state of Utah, rode the Conestoga wagons in his sleep. He came here from the sight of mountains "on which the gods of the Utes walked in the cool of the day.". In his mature life he must have made it back to lodestone once every twenty-four hours. What other writer, "spidering a length of web"—one of Marianne Moore's fine metaphors —has ever snared so much of vanguard, settler, soldier, Indian, Mormon, hunter, trapper, trader, greenhorn, varmint; wagon trains, encampments; fights, massacres, disasters, Laramies and Colorados; zions, rivers, prairies and revelations?

Benny's words were always arrows. Note the novelist turned historian: his character, Bill Bowen, this imaginary "settled citizen of Sangamon County or Brattleboro or the Mohawk Valley," pulling up his stakes. Note the New England background— Thoreau in his own voice, Melville in *Hyperboreans*; but always DeVoto who could say such things as "Parkman on the Indians is Parkman in the shadow of death."

Had the pond reflected the true glare of two-feet solid, our passage would have haled back Massachusetts' long lost art of harvesting what Ogden Nash calls "iceman's ice." Far better, though, that some stray reader, standing by this random acre in suburbia, should fancy that the Wasatch Mountains beckon in the distance, whence the wagons, the canal barge, glistening irons and the vapor trails each in their turn have borne away so quickly what New England of herself could spare.

188

WEDGE POND, WINCHESTER, MASSACHUSETTS

This was by far the easiest sunset picture I have ever taken. The location is only a mile from my home. I was shopping at the supermarket across Main Street when I saw this sunset building up. Fortunately I had my camera and tripod in my car. With sunsets it is difficult to judge the correct exposure or really to select the height of the brilliance in any one exposure. The best method is to shoot plenty before the sun goes down over the horizon and then wait for the afterglow, which could be best of all. I believe that this was about the fourth of a half dozen exposures. Thoreau wrote, "I have traveled a good deal in Concord." How many of us merit the rebut in his remark, "What a fool he is who thinks his Eldorado is anywhere but where he lives."

Exposure—1/5 of a second at f:11. ASA Speed 50.

ARTHUR GRIFFIN

And Round the World Away

The coast of Maine was in former years brought so near to foreign shores by its busy fleet of ships that among the older men and women one still finds a surprising proportion of travelers. Each seaward-stretching headland with its high-set houses, each island of a single farm, has sent its spies to view many a Land of Eshcol; one may see plain, contented old faces at the windows, whose eyes have looked at far-away ports and known the splendors of the Eastern world. They shame the easy voyager of the North Atlantic and the Mediterranean; they have rounded the Cape of Good Hope and braved the angry seas of Cape Horn in small wooden ships; they have brought up their hardy boys and girls on narrow decks; they were among the last of the Northmen's children to go adventuring to unknown shores. More than this one cannot give to a young State for its enlightenment; the sea captains and the captains' wives of Maine knew something of the wide world, and never mistook their native parishes for the whole instead of a part thereof; they knew not only Thomaston and Castine and Portland, but London and Bristol and Bordeaux, and the strange-mannered harbors of the China Sea.

SARAH ORNE JEWETT

Sarah Orne Jewett, who was graduated one hundred and one years ago from Berwick Academy in South Berwick, Maine, is sure of a lasting place in American letters. She lived and died in the house in which she was born. *The Country of the Pointed Firs* is a recognized classic; and her younger friend, the Nebraskan Willa Cather, believed that its security was just as predictable as that of *Huckleberry Finn* and *The Scarlet Letter*. Although the locale of Miss Jewett's novels and short stories centers on the southern coast of Maine, her voice is the right one—for me at least—to speak up for Boothbay Harbor.

Serene among her many books is *Country By-ways*; and the following excerpt from "A Mournful Villager" might well have drawn its inspiration from any coastal town on the whole Maine littoral. Miss Jewett is a master of sentiment which never slops over into sentimentality. There is, besides, great natural dignity in her writing; and readers who have missed her classic as well as such short stories as "A Dunnet Shepherdess," "A White Heron," "The Queen's Twin," and especially "Miss Tempy's Watchers" will at least note the cut of her jib in this long single paragraph:

I have received many kindnesses at my friends' hands, but I do not know that I have ever felt myself to be a more fortunate or honored guest than I used years ago, when I sometimes went to call upon an elderly friend of my mother who lived in most pleasant and stately fashion. . . . I can remember that I used to sit on a tall ottoman, with nothing to lean against, and my feet were off soundings, I was so high above the floor. We used to discuss the weather . . . and we tried to make ourselves agreeable to each other. Presently my lady would take her keys out of her pocket, and sometimes a maid would come to serve me, or else she herself would bring me a silver tray with some pound-cakes baked in hearts and rounds, and a small glass of wine, and I proudly felt that I was a guest, though I was such a little thing an attention was being paid me, and a thrill of satisfaction used to go over me for my consequence and importance. A handful of sugar-plums would have seemed nothing beside this entertainment. I used to be careful not to crumble the cake, and I used to eat it with my gloves on, and a pleasant fragrance would cling for some time afterward to the ends of the short Lisle-thread fingers. . . . It was not many years ago that I went to my old friend's funeral—and saw them carry her down the long, wide walk, between the tall box borders which were her pride . . . and the rows of her dear Dutch tulips stood dismayed in their flaunting colors and watched her go away.

(Sarah Orne Jewett)

192

BOOTHBAY HARBOR, MAINE

Alaska is almost the only state I haven't photographed. Somehow or other this scene is just about what I might expect to see in our forty-ninth state. Down Maine there used to be a saying that there are only two seasons in a year—winter and August. That may have been, but for photographers all seasons are great in New England's largest state. And perhaps the best part of the off season is that prices are lower and accommodations plentiful. With its 3000 miles of coastline you'll never run out of fishing villages or pounding seas to photograph.

Exposure—1/25 of a second at f:20. ASA Speed 50.

ARTHUR GRIFFIN

The Dawn Stone

The tops of mountains are among the unfinished parts of the globe, whither it is a slight insult to the gods to climb and pry into their secrets, and try their effect on our humanity. Only daring and insolent men, perchance, go there. Simple races, as savages, do not climb mountains,—their tops are sacred and mysterious tracts never visited by them. Pomola is always angry with those who climb to the summit of Ktaadn.

"Suppose," said [Thoreau to Joe Polis, his Oldtown Indian guide], "that I should take you in a dark night, right up here into the middle of the woods a hundred miles, set you down, and turn you round quickly twenty times, could you steer straight to Oldtown?" "Oh, yer," said he, "have done pretty much same thing. I will tell you. Some years ago I met an old white hunter at Millinocket; very good hunter. He said he could go anywhere in the woods. He wanted to hunt with me that day, so we start. We chase a moose all the forenoon, round and round, till middle of afternoon, when we kill him. Then I said to him, now you go straight to camp. Don't go round and round where we've been, but go straight. He said, I can't do that, I don't know where I am. Where you think camp? I asked. He pointed so. Then I laugh at him. I take the lead and go right off the other way, cross our tracks many times, straight camp." "How do you do that?" asked I. "Oh, I can't tell *you*," he replied. "Great difference between me and white man."

HENRY DAVID THOREAU

The forest primeval is best seen from the top of a mountain. It then impresses one by its extent, like an Oriental epic. To be in it is nothing, for then an acre is as good as a thousand square miles. You cannot see five rods in any direction, and the ferns, mosses, and tree-trunks just around you are the best of it. As for solitude, night will make a better one with ten feet square of pitch dark; and mere size is hardly an element of grandeur, except in works of man,—as the Colosseum. It is through one or the other pole of vanity that men feel the sublime in mountains. It is either, How small great I am beside it! or, Big as you are, little I's soul will hold a dozen of you. The true idea of a forest is not a selva selvaggia, but something humanized a little, as we imagine the forest of Arden, with trees standing at royal intervals,—a commonwealth, and not a communism. To some moods, it is congenial to look over endless leagues of unbroken savagery without a hint of man.

(James Russell Lowell)

James Russell Lowell is writing about the Moosehead country in 1853. But what he says concerning the forest primeval (Longfellow's phrase) is true today if only one can find the forest. Man still climbs, but not so fast, alas, as the trees are falling.

Most children of the future will have flown before they ever have the thrill of climbing their first mountain. This is a tragedy to me akin to ghost writing —signing what you did not compose: wings instead of boots or sneakers, an outboard instead of a paddle. The first memorable mountain I ever climbed was Chocorua in New Hampshire. I climbed it with John Bradley, my oldest Thoreauvian friend, while we were still in college; but neither of us ventured to put into words the sight that lay below us. John could do it now, were he alive. He could always write; and he thought deeply before he wrote. *Parade of the Living*, his first book (1929), is a little masterpiece of ingenuity. Or listen to this from *Patterns of Survival*: "Nature has never been known to return a life, an organ, or an attitude, once she has taken it away." See page 41. One of the oldest fossils known to man —perhaps the oldest—(a starfish) is named for him.

MOUNT KATAHDIN, MAINE

In April, while on an assignment in Millinocket for a national magazine, I decided to get up before dawn and try for a picture of Mt. Katahdin, where the first rays of the sun hit America. I drove twenty-five miles, over poor icy roads, before I found a clearing where I could see the summit. I set my camera on the tripod and waited for the rays to touch Katahdin. As I did I heard a rustling on my right. Suddenly a big black bear appeared. I think that he was as startled as I for he stood still. I left my camera and slowly backed towards my car and reached it. The bear sniffed at the tripod and then walked off. When he was far enough away I made this picture and got out of there. Mt. Katahdin (alt. 5267), the highest peak in Maine, has its base on the shore of Togue Pond which is 800 feet above sea level. From the base the mountain appears to be as high as some of the Rockies, which rise from a plateau 5000 to 7000 feet above sea level.

Exposure—1/25 of a second at f:14. ASA Speed 50.

ARTHUR GRIFFIN

SOURCES & BIBLIOGRAPHY

page

7   Beston: *Herbs and the Earth:* Doubleday & Co., New York, 1935; also Doubleday Dolphin edn. (paper).

13   Sewall: *Phaenomena Quaedam Apocalyptica ad Aspectum Novi Orbis Configurata,* Boston, 1697 & 1727.

16   Hawthorne: *The Heart of Hawthorne's Journals,* ed. by Newton Arvin: Houghton Mifflin Co., Boston, 1929; also Barnes & Noble paperback edn.

16   Dickinson: from *Jubilee: 100 Years of the Atlantic,* ed. by Edward Weeks & Emily Flint: Little, Brown & Co., Boston, 1957.

17   Dickinson: *Letters of Emily Dickinson,* ed. by Mabel Loomis Todd: Harper & Row Publishers, New York, 1931; also Grossett & Dunlap Universal edn. (paper).

21   Frost: *Complete Poems of Robert Frost:* Henry Holt & Co., New York, 1950.

25   Dunn: *Cloudman Hill Heritage:* Marion E. Dodd & the Hampshire Bookshop, Northampton, 1939.

29   Sergeant: *Willa Cather: A Memoir:* J. B. Lippincott Co., Philadelphia, 1953; Belmont Bison edn. (paper).

30   Thayer: *Louis Agassiz Fuertes,* ed. by Mary Fuertes Boynton: Oxford Univ. Press, Inc., New York, 1956.

33   Emerson: *Essays: Second Series*—"Nature"; included in *Essays and Other Writings,* ed. by Brooks Atkinson: Random House Modern Lib. (paper).

37   Sachs: *Modern Prints & Drawings,* selec. and ed. by Paul J. Sachs: Alfred A. Knopf, Inc., New York, 1954.

38   Whistler: *The Gentle Art of Making Enemies:* G. P. Putnam's Sons, New York, 1936.

41   Bradley: *Patterns of Survival: An Anatomy of Life:* The Macmillan Co., New York, 1936.

42   Henry: *Justin Morgan Had a Horse:* Follett Publishing Co., Chicago, 1945 (taken by Rand McNally).

45   Thoreau: *The Heart of Thoreau's Journals,* ed. by Odell Shepard: Houghton Mifflin Co., Boston, 1927; also Dover edn. (paper).

46   Brooks: *The Flowering of New England:* E. P. Dutton & Co., New York, 1936; also Dutton paper edn.

46   Hawthorne: *The Heart of Hawthorne's Journals,* ed. by Newton Arvin: Houghton Mifflin Co., Boston, 1929; also Barnes & Noble paperback edn.

49   Baedeker: *Baedeker's United States: 1909:* Charles Scribner's Sons, New York, 1909.

50   Constable: "Three Stars for Baedeker": *Harper's Magazine,* New York, April 1953.

53   Longfellow: *Complete Poetical Works,* ed. by H. E. Scudder: Houghton Mifflin Co., Boston, 1893 (in print).

57   Kipling: *Letters of Travel (1892-1913):* The Macmillan Co., New York, 1920.

62   Robinson: "The Man Against the Sky": see *Selected Poems,* ed. by Morton Dauwen Zabel: The Macmillan Co., New York.

67   Melville: *Moby Dick:* in Random House Modern Lib. edn., ill. by Rockwell Kent.

68   Trollope: *North America:* Chapman & Hall, London, 1862.

71   Slosson: *Story-Tell Lib:* Charles Scribner's Sons, New York, 1900.

72   Jewett: "A Mournful Villager," from *Country By-ways:* Houghton Mifflin Co., Boston, 1881.

75   Hine: *The Story of Martha's Vineyard,* ed. by C. G. Hine: Hine Bros., New York, 1908.

76   Shaler: *The Story of Martha's Vineyard,* ed. by C. G. Hine: Hine Bros., New York, 1908.

76   Burgess: from "The Old South Road of Gay Head": The Dukes County Hist. Soc., Edgartown, 1926.

79   Longfellow: *Complete Poetical Works,* ed. by H. E. Scudder: Houghton Mifflin Co., Boston, 1893 (in print).

80   Chase: *A Goodly Heritage:* Henry Holt & Co., New York, 1932.

83   Carson: *The Sense of Wonder:* Harper & Row Publishers, New York, 1965.

84   Beston: *The Outermost House:* Henry Holt & Co., New York, 1928; also Viking Compass edn. (paper).

87   Pratt: *Bill Pratt the Saw-Buck Philosopher* by John Sheridan Zelie & Carroll Perry, Williamstown, 1895 (privately printed).

91   Hathaway: *The Little Locksmith:* Coward-McCann, Inc., New York, 1942.

92   Jewett: *Country By-ways:* Houghton Mifflin Co., Boston, 1881.

95   Bradford: *Of Plymouth Plantation: 1620-1647,* ed. by Samuel Eliot Morison: Alfred A. Knopf, Inc., New York, 1952; also Putnam Capricorn edn. (paper).

96   Benét: *Western Star:* Henry Holt & Co., New York, 1943; also Doubleday Dolphin edn. (paper).

99   Beecher: *Star Papers:* J. C. Derby, New York, 1855.

103 Carson: *The Edge of the Sea:* Houghton Mifflin Co., Boston, 1955; also New Amer. Lib. Signet edn. (paper).

108 Brown: *I Travel by Train:* Appleton-Century, New York, 1939.

109 McCord: *The Crows:* Charles Scribner's Sons, New York, 1934.

113 Webster: *The Letters of Daniel Webster,* ed. by C. H. Van Tyne: McClure, Phillips Co., New York, 1902.

114 Thompson: *Fishing in New England:* The Chiswick Press, London, 1955.

117 Emerson: *Poems,* ed. by J. D. Adams: Crowell-Collier & Macmillan, New York, 1955. Also *Essays and Other Writings of Ralph Waldo Emerson,* ed. by Brooks Atkinson: Random House Modern Lib. edn. (paper).

121 Finley: "Traveling Afoot" from *The Art of Walking,* ed. by Edwin Valentine Mitchell: Loring & Mussey, New York, 1934; also in *The Pleasures of Walking:* Vanguard Press, Inc., New York, 1948.

125 Peattie: *Flowering Earth:* G. P. Putnam's Sons, New York, 1939; also Viking Compass edn. (paper).

126 Hill: from *The Harvard Book,* ed. by William Bentink-Smith: Harvard Univ. Press, Cambridge, 1953.

129 Pease: *Sequestered Vales of Life:* Harvard Univ. Press, Cambridge, 1946; also in *Waumbek Junction:* Gallows Hill Press, Cambridge, 1964.

133 Shepard: *Thy Rod and Thy Creel:* Dodd, Mead & Co., New York, 1931.

133 Greenslet: *Under the Bridge:* Houghton Mifflin Co., Boston, 1943.

134 McCord: *On Occasion:* Harvard Univ. Press, Cambridge, 1943.

137 Lewis: "The Man from Main Street" from *A Sinclair Lewis Reader,* ed. by Harry Mawle & Melville Caine: Random House, Inc., New York, 1953; also Pocket Books edn. (paper).

138 Frost: "New Hampshire" in *The Complete Poems of Robert Frost:* Henry Holt & Co., New York, 1950.

141 Richards: *A Northern Countryside:* Henry Holt & Co., New York, 1916; quoted in *White Pine and Blue Water: A State of Maine Reader,* ed. by Henry Beston: Farrar, Straus & Co., New York, 1950.

145 Cross: Yale Univ. Press, New Haven, 1937; from *As You Were,* ed. by Alexander Woollcott: Viking Press, New York, 1943.

146 Cogswell: "Extracts from the Diary of Dr. Mason Fitch Cogswell," ed. by Leonard Bacon: *The Connecticut Quarterly,* Hartford, 1899.

149 Perry: "Fishing With A Worm": *The Atlantic Monthly,* Boston, 1904; see also *Pools and Ripples,* by Bliss Perry: Little, Brown & Co., Boston, 1927.

154 Edwards: *Selected Shelburne Essays,* ed. by Paul Elmer More: Oxford Univ. Press, Inc., New York, 1935.

154 Price: "Amphion's Lyre," from *A Complete College Reader,* ed. by John Holmes & Carroll Towle: Houghton Mifflin Co., Boston, 1950.

154 Holmes: "A Soldier's Faith," from *A Commonplace Book,* by Charles P. Curtis: Simon & Schuster, Inc. New York, 1957.

154 Holmes: "Natural Law," from *Collected Legal Papers:* Peter Smith, Gloucester.

159 Thoreau: "Cape Cod": see *Walden and Other Writings,* ed. by Brooks Atkinson: Random House Modern Lib. edn.

159 Schlesinger: *A Thousand Days:* Houghton Mifflin Co., Boston, 1965.

163 Revere: "Paul Revere's Own Account of His Ride," from a letter to Jeremy Belknap, *Proc.,* 1879, ed. by Charles Deane.

164 Bancroft: "Battle of Lexington," reprinted from *New England Discovery,* ed. by Nancy Hale: Coward-McCann, Inc., New York, 1963.

167 Emerson: "Thoreau," see *Complete Essays & Other Writings:* Random House Modern Lib. edn. (paper).

168 Thoreau: *Walden & Other Writings,* ed. by Brooks Atkinson, Random House Modern Lib. edn. (paper).

171 Whittier: *The Complete Poetical Works:* Houghton Mifflin Co., Boston, 1894 (in print).

172 Thoreau: "A Winter Walk," see *Maine Woods:* College and Univ. Press, New Haven (paper).

175 Emerson: *Poems,* ed. by J. D. Adams: Crowell-Collier & Macmillan, New York, 1965.

176 Brooks: *The Flowering of New England:* E. P. Dutton & Co., New York, 1936; also Dutton paper edn.

179 Taber: *Stowe Notes:* Houghton Mifflin Co., Boston, 1913.

180 Beston: *The Outermost House:* Henry Holt & Co., New York, 1928; also Viking Compass edn. (paper).

183 Townsend: *Beach Grass:* Marshall Jones Co., Boston (but now of Francestown, N. H.), 1923.

187 DeVoto: *The Year of Decision: 1846:* Houghton Mifflin Co., Boston, 1950; also Houghton Mifflin Sentry edn. (paper).

188 DeVoto: *New England: There She Stands:* Harper's Magazine, New York, March, 1932; also in *Forays and Rebuttles,* by Bernard DeVoto: Little, Brown & Co., Boston, 1936.

191 Jewett: "The Queen's Twin," from *The Queen's Twin & Other Stories:* Houghton Mifflin Co., Boston, 1899.

192 Jewett: "A Mournful Village," from *Country By-ways:* Houghton Mifflin Co., Boston, 1881.

195 Thoreau: *The Maine Woods:* College and Univ. Press, New Haven (paper).

196 Lowell: *Literary Essays:* Houghton Mifflin Co., Boston, 1890.   (A B)

INDEX OF AUTHORS

200

LEE CLAIRE GRIFFIN   ABBOTT THAYER   CHARLES WENDELL

    DAVID McCORD   LESLIE P. THOMPSON   JOHN FITZGERALD K

HERMAN MELVILLE   HENRY DAVID THOREAU   NATHANIEL H

    ARTHUR STANLEY PEASE   EDWARD MARTIN TABER   RUDY

DONALD CULROSS PEATTIE   OLIVER WENDELL HOLMES, JR.

    ARTHUR GRIFFIN   BLISS PERRY   HENRY WADSWORTH LON

BILL PRATT   LUCIEN PRICE   ANTHONY TROLLOPE   SARAH O

    PAUL REVERE   RALPH WALDO EMERSON   JOHN HODGD

ROSALYND RICHARDS   JOHN FINLEY   ROBERT FROST   WILL

    EDWIN ARLINGTON ROBINSON   FERRIS GREENSLET   DA

PAUL J. SACHS   JONATHAN EDWARDS   KATHERINE BUTLER H

    ARTHUR M. SCHLESINGER, JR.   JAMES ABBOT McNEILL WHIST

ELIZABETH SHEPLEY SERGEANT   JOHN GREENLEAF WHITTIER

    NATHANIEL SOUTHGATE SHALER   MARGUERITE HENRY   H

ODELL SHEPARD   HENRY WADSWORTH LONGFELLOW   SINC

    ANNIE TRUMBULL SLOSSON   JAMES RUSSELL LOWELL